Ordination by Meer Presbyters Prov'd Void and Null. In a Conference Between Philalethes a Presbyter of the Church of England, and Pseudocheus a Dissenting Teacher

ORDINATION

BY

Meer Presbyters

PROV'D

VOID and *NULL.*

IN A

CONFERENCE

BETWEEN

PHILALETHES a *Presbyter* of the *Church* of *England,*

AND

PSEUDOCHEUS a *Dissenting Teacher.*

Verily, verily I say unto you; He that entreth not by the Door into the Sheepfold, but climbeth up some other Way, the same is a Thief and a Robber.
But he that entreth in by the Door, is the Shepherd of the Sheep, St. Joh. 10. 1, 2.

LONDON,

Printed by *J. L.* for W. FREEMAN, at the *Bible* over against the *Middle-Temple-Gate* in *Fleetstreet.*
M DCC VII.

To the WORSHIPFUL

AND MY

Much Honour'd FRIEND,

Hugh Smithſon, *Eſq;*

OF

Tottenham in *Middleſex*.

S I R,

NO *Sooner did I call to mind*
your hearty Zeal *for our*
moſt Excellent Church of
England, *and alſo your great* Integrity *which has been ſo very viſible in*
your indefatigable Endeavours *to*
promote *the* true Intereſt *of your*

Coun-

Country, but I ceas'd to debate any longer with my self, whose Name *I should borrow to* Patronize *my* Discourse. *This* Book, *Sir, which I now humbly Present to your View, is a* Conference *with a* Dissenting Teacher, *concerning the* Invalidity *of* Presbyterian Ordination. *And truly whensoever we make any Enquiries into the* Dissenters *pretended* Call, *we should do well to ask them the same* Question *concerning their* Mission, *that our* Blessed Saviour *ask'd the* Jews *concerning the* Baptism *of* St. John, Was it from Heaven, or of Men * ? *If these* Dissenting Teachers *shall say that their* Ordinations *were from Men, then they must produce their* Orders *from our* Diocesan

* St. Matth. 21 25.

Bishops,

Bishops, *who are the* Holy Apoftles Succeffors, *and who only have the* Power *of* Ordination : *If they fhall fay from* Heaven, *then they muft produce* unqueftionable Credentials *to convince us, that their* Call *was from the* Clouds, *like unto St.* Paul's, *when he was in his* Way *to* Damafcus. *And then if this could be perform'd, yet we live in fuch an Age of* Scepticifm, *that* Men *will not believe the Boaft of* Revelation, *without the Atteftation of a* Miracle. *And ferioufly, the* Chriftian World *is not to be blam'd for this fufpicious Humour ; for fo many* Impoftures *and* Delufions *have been impos'd upon Mankind by this* Pretence, *that 'tis a Prudence highly commendable not to be too too* Credulous. *So that feeing our* Se-

A 3 &taries

&taries *have no* Priesthood, *I do believe their* Conventicles *to be no more a* Church, *than any Number of* Merchants *that are met together upon the* Royal Exchange. For *tho' some of their* Congregations *may retain* Imposition of Hands *as a Mockery of* Ordination, *yet the* Imposing of Lay-Hands *has no more Power to confer* Priesthood, *than I have to constitute a* Judge *of* Oyer *and* Terminer.

Indeed, *Sir, I have a great* Compassion *for those* unstable *and* unwary Souls *among the* Dissenters, *that are perverted and drawn aside by these* Conventicle-Leaders, *and certainly the only Method to undeceive them, and to recover them into our* Establish'd Church, *is to* Prove (*as I have here done*)
that

that those very Persons, whom they take to be their Spiritual Guides, are no other than Impostors and Usurpers; and then if they have not surrender'd their Reason to their Deluding Teachers, and are not under any Pertinacious Resolutions, they must necessarily be convinc'd, that by their Schism and Separation, they are in a most Dangerous and Deplorable Condition: And much more Gloomy would their Apprehensions be, if they were but truly sensible, that God will most assuredly ratifie a Dif-union with the Bishop on Earth, by a like Dif-union in Heaven.

And now, Sir, I do very humbly beg your Pardon for prefixing your Name to this Discourse,

and

and if I have said any thing unworthy of your Patronage, *I know that as your* Judgment *will instantly discover it, so your great* Goodness *and* Candor *will freely forgive it ; since 'twas my* Duty *to our* Church, *and to its* excellent Governours *that prompted and encourag'd me to this Attempt.*

I shall add no more, but my most earnest Petitions *to the* Throne of Grace, *that the same* All-wise *and* Omnipotent God, *who has hitherto* Supported *and* Preserved you, *among all the* Changes *and* Chances *of this* mortal Life, *will be pleas'd to go on still to be* Gracious *unto you, to be your* Comfort, *and your exceeding great* Reward

ward *hereafter in the King-*
dom of Heaven; which shall be
the constant Prayer of,

Honour'd Sir,

Uxbridge,
Sept. 6.
1706.

Your most Faithful

and Humble Servant

JOHN JACQUES.

THE

THE
PREFACE.

THE Virulency of *Schifm* is reftlefs and implacable, and there is nothing fo apt to be revil'd and fpurn'd at as our moft *Excellent Church* and its *Sacred Conftitutions*. We muft therefore in thefe loofe and licentious Times of *Atheifm* and *Irreligion* guard and fortifie our felves with Courage and Refolution againft all *Calumnies* and *Contradictions* whatfoever. For *Satan* that *Arch-Enemy* of all Mankind, and the firft *Schifmatick* that ever was in the World, did not only by his *faucy Affectation* of a *Parity* with G O D caufe a *Divifion* and *Tumult* in Heaven, but he has alfo

alfo ftill his *Agents* and *Factors* to create the like *Differences* here Below; he infpirits them with a *fiery* and *malignant Zeal*, againft the *pureft Worfhip* and *Difcipline*, that fince the *Apoftolick Times* has appear-ed upon the Face of the Earth. And indeed there has been no Age fince the *Holy Apoftles* wholly free from *Schifmaticks* and *Impoftors*, but perhaps none ever aflorded fuch Swarms of them, as our unhappy Days, in which thefe *Sons of Craft* act under various Difguifes, and wheedle the People with their *pious Frauds*; they creep into Houfes, and lead Captive *filly Women* laden with divers Lufts; they beguile the weaker Sex, fway'd more by *Paffion* than by *Reafon*, and fo more eafily are feduc'd by them. Therefore we are exhorted by the *Holy Apoftle, To mark them that caufe Divifions, and to avoid them; for they ferve not the Lord Jefus Chrift but their own Belly, and with good Words and fair Speeches deceive*
the

the Hearts of the Simple. Rom. 6. 17.
So that he would have a *Mark* set
set upon *Schismaticks ,* that they
may be known and shun'd by all
Christians, as Persons of a very *Dangerous* and *Contagious Society.* Shall
we then, that are the *Watchmen* of
Israel, see *Schism* and *Faction* thrive
and prosper, and again to *Insult* the
best of Churches in the World, and
not endeavour to prevent their
Growth, and *spreading Infection?*
Shall not we give our People warning to avoid the *insnaring Temptations* of *Schism,* and shall not we
encourage them to *stand fast in the
Lord?* Shall not we strive to preserve them from all *Damnable Doctrines,* and to keep them stedfast
in their most *Holy Faith?* These
truly are our *great Duties,* which
if we did neglect, we should then
most shamefully betray the *Cause* of
our *Blessed Master,* and expose it to
the greatest *Obloquy* and *Contempt*
imaginable.

In

In the latter end of the Year
1692. My Neighbour *Pfeudocheus*
fent me a Letter, wherein he requir'd me to prove what I had faid
concerning the *Invalidity of Pref-
byterian Orders* ; becaufe he was
inform'd by one of his Hearers,
that I had afferted the *Miniftry* of
all *Nonconformifts* to be *Invalid* and
Null, who had not receiv'd *Epifcopal Ordination.*   At this time **I**
was engag'd in many urgent Affairs, and had only leifure to return him a very Friendly *Epiftle* ;
part of which was fome few *Col-
lections* from an Excellent Difcourfe
of a Celebrated Champion for the
Epifcopal Caufe *, wherein was a
plain Proof of this Pofition, *That
it was never in the Power of Meer
Presbyters to admit into the Miniftry by Impofition of Hands in Ordination.*   Then to thefe I added fe-

* *Bp.* Moffom *on Matth.* 28. 19, &c.

veral

veral pertinent and neceſſary *Ob-*
ſervations, as alſo an *Admonitory*
Concluſion. Now my ſole Deſign
in ſending him this *Epiſtle* was for
his particular Information and Re-
covery from *Schiſm,* but *Intùs ex-*
iſtens prohibet aliundè adveniens,
That which is got in already, keeps
out better, which ſhould come in
its Place;

> *Non benè conveniunt nec in una ſe-*
> *de morantur*
> *Majeſtas & Amor.*————Ovid.

The *Majeſty* of *Grace* and the *Fond-*
neſs of *Gain,* do not well agree
together, nor cohabit in the ſame
Breaſt. The inordinate Love of
Self-Intereſt is ſo predominant in
our *Diſſenting Teachers,* and does
ſo powerfully fence off all *Convi-*
ctions of *Conſcience,* that unleſs the
Grace of *God* did act irreſiſtibly,
they will never be convinc'd of
their *Damnable Sin,* even the *Uſur-*
pation

pation of the *Miniſterial Office.*
What ſaith the *Holy Apoſtle?* The
Natural Man, (for not one of theſe
can be ſaid to be *Spiritual*) ὖ δἒ-
χεται, *does not receive the things of
the Spirit of God,* 1 *Cor.* 2. 14. he
has not any Inclination for them,
and therefore will never be brought
to entertain them.   And truly ſuch
a *perverſe Spirit* does preſide in
this ſort of Men, that all Advices
of this Nature do but rather tend
to fire and inflame them; for after
that *Pſeudocheus* had receiv'd my
Letter, inſtead of ſhewing that *Gra-
titude,* which was due to my *cha-
ritable Endeavours,* he ſent me a
rude and *indigeſted Anſwer,* which
conſiſteth of ſuch *nauſeous Repeti-
tions, inexcuſable Blunders, forced*
and *fallacious Inferences,* that they
are all of them very obvious to a-
ny Perſons Underſtanding.   Theſe
were the ſmall *Velitations,* that
then paſs'd betveen us, which for
Ten Years and more have lain in
Ob-

Obfcurity, and why they were reviv'd and thruſt out into the World,
I can conceive no other Reaſon but
this. At a late *Conference,* after
other various Diſcourſes, we at the
laſt began to have ſome *warm De-
bates* upon our former Controver-
ſie; but before we had half can-
vas'd the Matter, or brought the
Point to any ſort of Concluſion,
our *Pamphleteer* was ſo wretchedly founder'd and bewilder'd, that
he had nothing farther to urge in
his own Vindication; nay, inſtead
of *defending* he *deſerted his Cauſe,*
and *Proteus*-like, he turn'd *Inde-
pendent,* and ſtraightway aſſerted,
*That the Suffrage of the People qua-
lify'd any Perſon to Preach the Holy Goſpel, and to Adminiſter the
Holy Sacraments without Ordination* *. At this *Conference* of ours,
ſeveral Perſons were preſent of both
Congregations; and the Report they

* *This will be atteſted by the Rev. Mr. C. G——k.*

made

made of it (as far as I can find)
was faithful and true; which no
sooner reach'd his Ears, and some
others of his *Party*, but *Choler* and
Spight appear'd very visible in their
Faces; and according to the Pro-
phet, *The shew of their Countenance
did witness against them*, *Isa.* 3. 9.
And thus they continu'd under
some strange *Confusions* and *Per-
plexities* of *Mind*, till such time
as they came to this Resolution,
that the only way to aggrieve me,
was to Print all those *Letters*, which
had formerly pass'd between us.
But instead of being disgusted by
the *Publication* of those *Letters*, I
am rather oblig'd by it; for now
he has given me a fair Opportuni-
ty to vindicate what I then wrote
from his *false Glosses* and *corrupt
Interpretations.* * The *Preface* to
his Book begins with many *specious*

---

* *See a Pamphlet entitled,* Some Letters concerning the
Validity of Ordination by Presbyters, *&c. by* J. W——s.
Sold by John Lawrence *at the* Angel *in the* Poultry, London.

Pretences to *Peace* and *Unity*; but what *Truth* can there be in such fair *Speeches*, or what Regard can be given to his *Words*, when his *Practices* at the same time confute them ? He can never be one of the *Sons of Peace*, but an avow'd, profefs'd, and downright *Enemy* unto it, in endeavouring to deſtroy, what he would be thought to preſerve: 'Tis a *meer Deluſion*, and a *Ridiculous Sham* to cry *Peace*, *Peace*, when at the ſame Time this *Adverſary* of ours has entred the *Liſts*, and made himſelf ready for *Battel*. In this, and many other particulars, you may clearly diſcern the *Spirit* of the Man; For can he ever be inclin'd to *repair* our *Breaches*, and *heal* our *Diviſions*, when all the while he is making of *Parties* to *widen* and *increaſe* them ? Can he be deſirous to promote *Peace* and *Unity* among *Proteſtants*, when at the ſame time he draws as many as ever he can in-

to the fame *Schifm* and *Separation*
with himfelf? No certainly, for all
his *Pretences* are juft like the *Po-
licies* of the *Algerines,* who moft
defign the *Slavery* of *Chriftians,*
when they hang out *Chriftian Co-
lours.* But after all his *glorious
Breathings* towards *Peace* and *Unity,* is it not ftrange that this *Adverfary* of mine fhould turn fuch
an *Accufer* of the *Brethren*? His
Words are thefe; * *But alas! Such
narrow-Soul'd Creatures are fome,
and fo addicted to their own Party, that they will hardly allow any
to be Chriftians in this Kingdom,
that are not conftant Members of
their* Englifh Catholick Church, *nor
own thofe as Brethren in the Miniftry (either here or in Forein
Parts) who were not* Ordain'd *by
the Hands of* Diocefans. Now this
grand Partiality I have always obferv'd in the *Presbyterians* them-

* *See the Preface to the faid Book, p.* 2.

felves,

felves, who would never vouchſafe the Title of *good Chriſtian* to any Perſon, unleſs he was one of their own *Denomination :* And as the *old Donatiſts* confin'd the Limits of the Church, *in Angulo & particula Africæ,* in a corner and ſmall part of *Africa ;* ſo our *new Engliſh* ones do impale the *true Church* of *Chriſt* within their own *Party.* Theſe, theſe are the *Godly,* the *Brethren,* the *Precious,* the *Children of God ;* for all others are reputed *unſavoury Salt, Miſerable Caſt-aways,* and *Abominable Barbarians.* But is this the true and genuine *Spirit* of *Chriſtianity ?* Is it not rather the *Spirit* of *Bigottry* and *Infatuation ?* And is not this *Pſeudocheus* acted by the very ſame *Spirit ?* He accuſeth me of *unhappy Principles,* and no leſs *unhappy Temper,* which made me to attempt the *blaſting* of his *Miniſtry* (as he calls it) without any Provocation on his Part. *Good Man !* Is it no Provocation to an *Eſtabliſh'd*

Cler-

Clergyman to fee the *Gathering of Churches out of Churches,* and the *fetting up of Altar againft Altar?* Is it no Provocation to fee *Pfeudocheus* ufing all his little *Arts* and *Devices* to draw *Difciples* after him, to increafe his *Party,* and to fill up his *Conventicle?* He would do well to perufe that *Presbyterian* Book, Entitled, * *Jus Divinum Regiminis Ecclefiaftici,* and there he will be inform'd, That this Practice of *Gathering Churches out of Churches,* and of fetting up *feparate Meetings* againft an *Eftablifh'd Church,* is bitterly inveigh'd againft, as the *Mother of Confufion,* and the *Nurfe of Schifm.* This was a thing that was feverely condemn'd by the *Puritans* of old, in the *Brownifts ;* and by the *Presbyterians* of late, in the *Independents,* and other *Sectaries :* But in thefe Days of ours, wherein *Religion* becomes *Tributary* to *Intereft,* the Na-

---

* *A Book made by the* London *Minifters, Ann.* 1647.

ture

ture of *Schifm* muft not be laid open and expos'd, becaufe *Pfeudocheus*'s *Conventicle* is founded upon it. If the tender Points of *Divifion*, fo fharply rebuk'd by the *Holy Apoftle*, be fo much as touch'd upon in any of my publick or private *Difcourfes*, no fooner does he hear of them, but he prefently calls them my *Infolent Clamours*. If I inform the People, that the *Diffenters* induftrious way of making *Profelytes* is not to the *Embracing* of *Chriftianity*, and to the *true Practice* of *Piety* and *Vertue*; but to a *Party*, a *Faction*, a *Schifm* and *Separation* from an *Eftablifh'd Church*; then this tefty *Smectymnuan* *, calls me an *Incendiary*. Thus he *Hath given his Mouth to* Evil, *and his Tongue frameth Deceit*; and he appears to be wholly directed by that pernicious Maxim, *Calumniare fortiter, & aliquid adhærebit*, Slander ftoutly, and fomething will ftick behind. Do but

---

* So call'd from *Steph. Marfhall, Edm. Calamy, Tim. Young, Matt. Newcomen, Will. Spurftow.*

obe

obferve the many *rancorous Infinua-tions* and *Mifreprefentations* through out his whole *Preface* ; but thefe be-ing his own *Brain-fick Conjectures,* are all of them *notorioufly falfe,* and to his *Conviction* and *Shame* they have been already prov'd fo.   Is it then fo very natural to our *Diffen-ters* to promote their own *Intereft* and *wily Defigns* by *odious Falfities* and *flanderous Criminations?* Does *Fanaticifm* ftand in need of fuch *im-pious Forgeries,* and muft *Pfeudoche-us* talk fo *deceitfully* for its *Advance-ment?* If fo, then here the *Cenfure* muft fall ; That 'tis certainly a very *ftrong Prefumption* of a moft *weak* and *feeble Caufe,* when the *Refuge* and *Support* of it are *Impudent* and *Audacious Lies.*

Thus I have done with my *Adver-fary's Preface,* and fhall now pro-ceed to the *Conference* it felf, where-in the *Reader* will find, That *Ordi-nation by Meer Presbyters is prov'd Void and Null* ; That *Diocefan Epi-fcopacy*

fcopacy is an *Apoſtolick,* and confe-
quently a *Divine Inſtitution*; and
that all *Pſeudocheus*'s *poor Objections*
againſt it are utterly *overthrown* and
deſtroy'd. What then remains afterwards is, to advife all good *Chriſtians*, as they tender their *everlaſting
Salvation*, moſt carefully to avoid all
Schiſmaticks and their *pernicious
Principles*, and to renounce all manner of *Communion* with fuch *falſe*
and *counterfeit Miniſters*; and if I
am thought to be too *plain* and *free*
in this my *Advice* to a *loofe* and *licentious Age*, I fhall be fure to continue fo, whenfoever I find an occafion: and tho' perhaps I may offend
fome *nice* and *captious* Ears, and ex-
afperate thofe whom I do oppofe,
that's none of my Fault, but theirs;
For none fhould be *offended* at the
Truth, and he that is *exaſperated*
and *enrag'd* by it, difcovers a *malignant* and *ulcerated Mind.*

T H E

THE
CONTENTS.

The CONTENTS.

Επισ-

The CONTENTS.

Yet

The CONTENTS.

The CONTENTS.

Juſt Publiſh'd,

THeſaurarium Mathematicæ, or the Treaſury of the Mathematicks Containing variety of uſeful Practices in Arithmetick, Geometry, Trigonometry, Aſtronomy Geography, Navigation and Surveying; as alſo the Menſuration of Board, Glaſs, Tiling, Paving, Timber, Stone, and Irregular Solids. Likewiſe it teacheth the Art of, Gauging, Dialling, Fortification, Military Orders and Gunnery· Explains the Logarithms, Sines, Tangents and Secants· Sheweth their Uſe in Arithmetick, &c. To which is annex'd a Table of 10000 Logarithms, Log-Sines and Log-Tangents. Illuſtrated with ſeveral Mathematical Sculptures on Copper-Plates Originally Compos'd by J. Taylor, Gent And now carefully Reviſed and Corrected. To which is added, the Uſe and Practice of ſeveral Propoſitions and Problems throughout the whole Work, as alſo the Deſcription and Uſe of both Globes, and ſome of the chiefeſt Mathematical Inſtruments both for Sea and Land. With many other conſiderable Additions and Improvements. By W. Alingham, Teacher of the Mathematicks.

Lately Publiſh'd,

The Devout Communicant, exemplified in his Behaviour Before, At and After the Sacrament of the Lords-Supper, Practically ſuited to all the Parts of that Solemn Ordinance. The Ninth Edition Price 1s. 6d.

The Whole Duty of a Chriſtian. Containing all things neceſſary both as to what he is to Know and Do for obtaining a happy Eternity Price 1s. 6d.

An Infallible way to Contentment, in two Parts compleat. Price 2s.

The Anatomy of the Earth, mention'd in the Catalogue at the end of this Book, is Price 6d.

All Printed for W. Freeman, againſt the Middle-Temple-Gate, Fleetſtreet.

ORDI-

ORDINATION

BY

𝕸𝖊𝖊𝖗 𝕻𝖗𝖊𝖘𝖇𝖞𝖙𝖊𝖗𝖘

PROV'D

VOID and NULL.

Philalethes.   *Pseudocheus.*

Phil. WHAT Right can you pretend to the *Name* and *Office* of a *Presbyter*, *Pseudocheus*, who have not receiv'd Imposition of Hands from a Lawful Authority, and so not duly distinguish'd from the rest of Mankind to serve in the Offices

B   of

of *Religion* ' From whom did you receive your *Mission* ? If you fay from *Jefus Chrift* and his Holy Apoftles , Give me then leave to ask you whether *Immediately* , or *Mediately* ? *Immediately* you will not fay ; If *Mediately,* then I defire to be inform'd by whom, or from whofe Hands you did receive your *Mission* ? You could not receive *Orders* from the *Presbyters* of the Church of *England* ; for the Power of *Ordaining* was never convey'd to them, and fo by them could never be tranfmitted to any others. Since then you cannot derive any *Ordination* from the *Presbyters* of the Church of *England,* you muft of neceffity produce fome one *Church* founded by the Holy Apoftles , whofe Chief Governour was no other than a *Meer Presbyter* ; Then you muft prove a conftant and uninterrupted Succeffion of fuch *Governing-Presbyters* in that Church down to thefe very Times ; Then
you

you muſt prove that from them you have receiv'd your own *Miſſion :* Now if ſuch an *Eſtabliſhment* and *Succeſſion* cannot be found, you will never be able to prove that you ever receiv'd any *Ordination :* For the leaſt Failure or Defect in this *Succeſſion* utterly deſtroys the very *Being* of ſuch a *Presbyterian Church,* which can lay no manner of Claim to that Promiſe of our Bleſſed Saviour, which he made to his Holy Diſciples immediately before his Aſcenſion into Heaven, to ſecure his *Church* from *Error* and *Defection ; And lo I am with you alway even unto the End of the World. Matth.* 28. 20. 'Tis confeſs'd on all Hands, that a Man cannot Exerciſe the *Office* of a *Miniſter* without a *Call,* and ſince that you never had a *Lawful Ordinary Call,* I hope you will not pretend to one that was *Extraordinary ;* for that would be no leſs than *Enthuſiaſm,* unleſs you could make it apparent by your *Miracles,* and *Gift of Tongues.* B 2 *Pſeu.*

Pfeud. **Pray,** Philalethes, ^ᵗ *What is to be esteem'd a lawful Call, and what Ordination is requisite to invest a Man in this Office?*

Phil. There are Two Things requir'd in a *Lawful Call* and *Ordination* into the *Miniftry.*

1. That the *Clergy,* after a *previous Examination* of their *Abilities,* and *probable Teftimonies* concerning their *Sober Converfation,* fhall be Solemnly admitted into the *Miniftry* by *Prayer* and *Impofition of Hands.*

2. That the *Clergy* fhall be admitted by a *Lawful Authority.*

Firft. Every *Clergy-Man* muft be admitted into *Holy Orders* by *Prayer* and *Impofition of Hands.*

Our Bleffed Lord commanded his Holy Difciples to *Pray* immediately before he made them *Apoftles, Matth.* 9. 38. and *Chap.* 10. 1. And afterwards *Deacons* and others were

---

: Mr. *J. W.* Letters, p. 12.

Ordain'd by *Fasting*, *Prayer*, and *Imposition of Hands*, *Acts* 6. 6. and *Chap.* 14. 23. And this *Pious Custom* has been ever since continu'd in all the several Ages of the *Christian Church*, because it was begun by our Blessed Saviour and his Apostles. And 'tis very certain that every sort of *Power*, whether *Ecclesiastical*, *Civil*, or *Military*, ought always to be convey'd from one to another, by some *Solemn Creation*, *Admission*, or *Investiture* to the same.

Secondly. The *Clergy* shall be admitted into the *Ministry* by a *Lawful Authority.*

Diocesan Bishops are the only *Authority* that can admit into *Holy Orders*; And here I shall not only prove this by the XXIIId. Article of the *Church of England*, and the *Statute Laws* of the Realm, which say, *That no Man can be a Lawful* Priest *or* Deacon, *unless he be* Ordain'd *by a* Bishop (*a*); But I will

____

(*a*) *Stat.* 13 *Eliz. c.* 12. § 1. *& Act of Uniform.* 14 *Car.* 2.

B 3   fur-

further fhew, that this *Law* is grounded upon *Holy Scripture*, and the *Canons* and *Practice* of the *Univerfal Church*. Firſt, Our Bleſſed Lord, as *Supreme Governour* of his *Church*, call'd and *ordain'd* his *Apoſtles* (*b*), and they *ordain'd* *Deacons*, *Presbyters* and *Biſhops* (*c*), but they gave the *Power* of admitting all others only to the *Biſhops*, to whom alſo they only gave Rules to direct them in examining and approving the *Candidates* for *Holy Orders* (*d*), and charg'd them to *Ordain* none haſtily; that is, not till they had thoroughly try'd them (*e*). And ſince there are no ſuch Rules in all St. *Paul*'s Epiſtles, but in thoſe that are directed to *Timothy* and *Titus*; it is a plain Demonſtration, that the Holy Apoſtle did intend, not only the *Ordination*, but

---

(*b*) *Matth.* 10. 1, 2. *ch.* 28. 19, 20. *Mar.* 3. 14. (*c*) *Act.* 6. 6. *&.* 14. 23. 2 *Tim.* 1. 6.   (*d*) 1 *Tim.* 3. 1, *&c.Tit.* 1. 5, *&c.*   (*e*) 1 *Tim.* 5. 22. *i. e.* Μὴ ἐκ πρώτης δοκιμασίας, μηδὲ ἐκ τρίτης ἀλλὰ πολλάκις ἐξετάσας ϗ ἀκριβῶς. Ita **Theophil.** in loc.

the

the *Scrutiny* and *Approbation* of a'' *Ecclefiaftical Officers*, fhould be fo'' ly in the *Bifhop*'s *Power*. The Apo- ftolical *Canons* are very exprefs, that two or three *Bifhops* are neceflary to the *Confecrating* a *Bifhop*, and one to the *Ordaining* a *Prieft* and *Deacon* (*f*) ; Neither of which, as *Dionyfius* obferves, can be initiated without the *Bifhop*'s *Prayer* (*g*). 'Tis uncertain how Ancient thefe *Canons* are, but *Blondel* grants that they were extant at leaft in the Third Age (*h*); and the Author of them does feem to have reduc'd into that one *Body* the former *Rules* and *Cu- ftoms* of the *Apoftolick Churches*. The Learned *Daille'*, the great *Pa- tron* of *Presbytery*, did acknowledge *Ordination* in St. *Cyprian*'s time was peculiarly the *Bifhop*'s *Right* (*i*): So that this *Confeffion* of fo great

---

(*f*) *Can. Apoftol.* 1. *&* 2. (*g*) *Dionyf. Ecclef. Hierar. cap.* 5 (*h*) *Blondel. Apolog pro Hieron. p.* 157. (*i*) *Or- dinationem* ——— *Epifcopalis juri. ifius fuiffe in Cyprianici feculi Ecclefia confitemur.* Daillé *de cult. Lat. Relig. lib.* 2. *cap.* 13. *p.* 17..

an *Adverfary* may excufe any further *Proof* for that Age; and if it
be confider'd, that the *Bifhops* down
from the *Holy Apoftles* to St. *Cyprian*'s Days were very *poor* and *perfe-
cuted*, as well as very *pious*, it cannot be thought they fhould have *u-
furp'd* any *Authority* which was not
left them by the *Holy Apoftles*. And
'tis very evident that thofe good Primitive *Bifhops*, the great *Propaga-
tors* of our *Chriftian Religion*, did
affume this *Power*, and the *Priefts*,
Deacons and *Laity* did yield an en-
tire *Obedience*; wherein that the
one did wrongfully *ufurp*, and the
other did weakly *comply*, is neither
probable nor *juft* to fuppofe.

Pfeud. *You have told me*, Philalethes, *What is to be efteem'd a* Lawful
Call, *and what* Ordination *is requifite to inveft a Man in the* Sacred Office *of the* Miniftry; *Now though we*
Diffenting Teachers *cannot pretend
to fuch a* Regular Call *and* Ordination, *as you have juft now defcribed*,
                                    yet

yet we do not look upon our felves as Ufurpers *of the* Minifterial Function, *but as true* Minifters, *and we are all of us fo careful and ftrict to prevent* * Herefies *and* Schifms, *Errors and Impieties from infecting or troubling the* Church, *by the Rafhnefs of* bold Intruders ; *that we allow not thofe to be* Seeds-Men *amongft us,* who either on one Side ignorantly pretend to the Spirit, *or on the other, fhall dare to deny his* Office, *or mock at his* Operations.

Phil. Thefe are fpecious *Pretences, Pfeudocheus,* yet when they come under an *impartial Scrutiny,* there will not appear the leaft Shadow of *Truth* or *Sincerity* in them ; For I'll plainly prove, that the *Diffenting Teachers,* who were *Ordain'd* by *Meer Presbyters,* are all of them *Ufurpers* of the *Minifterial Office:* But before I proceed upon that Head, I muft make a few *Remarks*

‡ Mr. *J. W's.* Letters, *p.* 12, 13.

con-

concerning that great *Care* and *Strictness*, which you so mightily boast of, in preventing *Heresies* and *Schisms*, Errors and Impieties from infecting and troubling the *Church* by the Rashness of *bold Intruders*. Certainly your *Party* has but small Reason to *Glory* in such *Noble Endeavours* ; How frequently have *Dissenters* been impos'd upon by *Romish Emissaries* in their very *Conventicles* ? Not only *Faithful Commin* and *Thomas Heth*, the one a *Dominican Friar*, and the other a *Jesuit*, * but many more in these latter Days have acted the Parts of *Dissenting Teachers*, and Preach'd in your *Conventicles* : That *Whitebread* and *Gavan*, who were Executed in the time of the *Popish Plot*, have frequently Preach'd in *Conventicles* in *Southwark*, and other Places ; and that the said *Whitebread, alias White*, did Preach in a *Presbyterian Conven-*

* *Foxes and Firebrands.*

ticle

ticle at *Spaldwick* near *Huntingdon*;
and that *Wright, Morgan* and *Ire-
land,* who were in *Romish Orders,*
did Preach in *Scotland* under the
Notion of *Presbyterian Teachers,*
are notorious and unquestionable
Truths. For if a *Jesuit* can bring
a *Counterfeit Letter* of *Recommen-
dation* from any remarkable *Diffen-
ter,* or if he does but get a *Certifi-
cate* that he has Preach'd in such or
such *Congregations,* with their *Approbation,* which he is sure to have,
if he inveighs against *Popery, Bishops, Ceremonies, Common-Prayer,*
and sets up for *Liberty of Consci-
ence,* his Business is instantly done,
and without any further *Scrutiny,*
he is admitted to *Hold Forth,* and
he is straightway applauded by such
undiscerning *Auditors* for a most
zealous Protestant, a *powerful* and
right Heavenly Man. Whereas the
Church of *England* takes Care that
none be admitted to the *Charge* of
Souls, without all the *Caution* imaginable

ginable againſt *Popery* ; The *Clergy*
of that *Church* muſt take the *Oaths*
appointed to be taken by *Law* ; they
muſt have *Teſtimonials* from Perſons
that know them, of their *Ability*
and *Soundneſs of Judgment*, they
muſt ſhew their *Letters of Ordination*, before they are admitted
to Preach in any unknown *Congregation*, and they muſt have a
Licenſe from the *Biſhop* of the *Dioceſe*, before they can regularly
Preach in a *Congregation*, whereunto by *Law* they are Inſtituted and
Inducted. If then the Care of your
Teachers had been as great to preſerve your People from *Error*, as their
Endeavours have been to keep them in
Ignorance, they would have been leſs
culpable and *pernicious*. And why was
you, *Pſeudocheus*, ſo *treacherous* to
the *Souls* of your poor *deluded Followers*, as to prevent any *Information* that might have brought them to
the *Knowledge* of the *Truth?* It was
but lately that a certain Perſon, who
was

was then one of your own *Party*, but is now of our *Communion*, did put into your Hands a *Book* containing feveral *Reafons* againft *Occafional Conformity*, and thereupon did requeft your *Opinion*; but you like a *Faithful Paftor*, after you had perus'd it, return'd it to him again with this particular *Caution*, *That by no means he muft fhew it to any Perfons of your Congregation.* Was not this, *Pfeudocheus*, a plain fymbolizing with *Popery?* For you endeavour to keep your *Followers* in *Ignorance* by the fame *Methods* the *Romifh Priefts* do theirs.

Pfeud. *Come, come,* Philalethes, *How will you prove the* Diffenting Teachers *that were* Ordain'd by Meer Presbyters *to be* Ufurpers *of the* Minifterial Office, *and that their* Ordinations *are* Invalid *and* Null? *We do fuppofe* * *that* Presbyters *cannot* Regularly admit *into the* Miniftry

---

* Mr. *J. W's Letters,* p. 13, 14.

by

by Ordination ; *yet it will not follow hence, that none fo admitted are true* Minifters, *nor that their* Ordination *is therefore* Invalid *and* Null. *For oftentimes (according to that old Maxim,* Quod fieri non debet, factum valet *) That which ought not to have been done, as being* Irregular, *yet being done, ought not to be annull'd for want of fome fit* Circumftances.

Phil. Would ever any Man, but you, *Pfeudocheus,* produce this *Maxim,* to prove the *Validity of Presbyterian Orders ?* All *Antiquity* will not afford one Inftance of *Presbyters* making Or*dinations* without a *Bifhop* ; If any *Presbyters* did claim a *Right* to Or*dain,* and did prefume againft the *Rule* of the *Church* in that particular, the *Church* of thofe times did declare their Or*dinations Null*, and thought that *Antichrift* was near at hand, when fuch new and unprefidented *Confufions* were permitted to arife. What *Sentence* fhall

fhall we think would they have pronounc'd upon *Presbyterian Or-dinations*, when they did not only refcind *Orders* conferr'd by *Bifbops*, againft the *Canons* and *Eftablifh'd Difcipline* of the *Church* (*k*), but in fome Cafes did *Re-ordain* (*l*)? If a confiderable *Party* of the *Scot-tifh* Laity, difliking fome Practices of the prefent *Kirk*, and attempt-ing (as they thought) a purer *Re-formation*, fhould take upon them to *Ordain Paftors* in their feparate *Congregations*, in oppofition to the receiv'd *Difcipline* fettled in their *General Synods*, I would appeal to you, or any *Teachers* in thofe *Churches*, Whether you or they held fuch an *Ordination* valid. This, *Pfeudocheus*, I take to be your own Cafe, and cannot but tell you, that not only fuch as thefe, but all o-ther *Irregular Ordinations* have been ever accounted as *Nullities*, for

(*k*) *Can. Nic* 9, 10, 16. *Can. Ant.* 73. (*l*) *Nic. Can.* 19

which

which feveral have been depriv'd of
Holy Orders, and reduc'd to a *Lay-
Communion.* In the *Council* of *Sar-
dica,* thofe *Clerks,* that were *Ordain'd* by *Mufæus* and *Eutychianus,*
who were not *Bifhops,* but only
two *Grecian Presbyters,* were redu-
ced to the State and Condition of
Laicks (m). The like *Decree* alfo
was made about the *Ordination* of
Maximus, a pretended, but no real
Bifhop, that the Perfons fhould be
reputed no *Clergymen,* and all his
Acts annull'd (*n*). So it was determin'd in a *Synod* at *Alexandria,*
by the famous Confeffor *Hofius* and
other *Bifhops* there affembled, That
Ifchyras who was *Ordain'd* by one
Colluthus a *Meer Presbyter,* fhould
be depriv'd of that *Degree* to which
he had falfly pretended (*o*), for
(fay they) fince *Colluthus* died but

(*m*) *Concil. Sardic. Can.* 18, 19. *Bev. Tom.* 1. *p.* 505.
(*n*) Μήτε τὰς πὰρ αὐτῶ Χειϱοτονηθέντας ἐν ὅιω δήποτε βαθμῶ κλήϱυ,
&c. *Concil. Conft.* 2. *Can.* 4. *Bev. T.* 1. *p.* 91. *Soz. lib.* 1. *c.* 9.
(*o*) Ἐκπεσῶν ἢ τῆς ψευδῆ ὑπονοίας τῦ πϱεσβυτεῖκ. *Synod. Alex-
and. ap. Athanaf. Apol.* 2.

a

a *Presbyter*, all his *Ordinations* are void *(p)*. The Council of *Hifpalis* degraded a *Priest* and two *Deacons* for this only Reaſon; Becauſe the Biſhop of *Agabra* being afflicted with Sore Eyes, and having ſome preſented to him to be *Ordain'd Presbyters* and *Deacons*; did only lay his Hands upon them, ſuffering a *Presbyter* that ſtood by to ſay the *Prayers* over them, and read the Words of *Ordination (q)*. This being conſider'd in the aforeſaid *Council*, upon Mature Deliberation it was thus determin'd. Firſt, The *Presbyter* that aſſiſted, for his Boldneſs and Preſumption, he had been ſubject to the *Council's Cenſure*, but that he was before Deceas'd: Next, The *Presbyter* and *Deacons*, who were ſo *Ordain'd*, ſhould be actually *depoſed* from all *Sacred Orders*; concluding thus, *Tales enim meritò judicati ſunt removendi, quia pravè*

<hr>

(p) Epiſt. Synodal. ap. Bin. T. 1. p. 405. (q) Concil. Hiſpal. 2. Can. 5. An. 619. Bin. T. 2. par. 2. p. 326.

inventi funt conftituti; that they were worthily adjudg'd to lofe their *Orders*, which they had wrongfully receiv'd. So little *Influence* had the *Presbyters* in the *Effential Parts* of *Ordination*, as that their bare Reading of the Words (though requir'd to it by the *Bifhop*) was adjudg'd enough, not only to make them liable to the *Church's Cenfure*, but alfo for their Sakes to make void the *Action*. I could produce other *Examples* of this Nature, but thefe may fuffice to let you fee, what were the Effects of fuch *Irregular Ordinations*, they were accounted as *Nullities*, tho' perform'd by thofe who were in *Sacred Orders*.

Pfeud. [*] *I could give you many Inftances to clear the Truth of what I have before afferted, but I fhall content my felf at prefent with this one, which is* ad Hominem *and clofe to*

***

[*] Mr. *J. W*'s *Letters*, p. 14.

the purpose. Lay-men *have not Power to* Baptize. *Now tho' you esteem us, who were not* Ordain'd *by* Diocesans, *to be no* true Ministers *but* Lay-men : *Yet you do not* Re-Baptize *any of those who had been* Baptized *by us, but admit them to the* Lord's-Supper *, without questioning their former* Baptism *as Invalid. If you say that* Lay-men *have Power to* Baptize; *prove that, and by the same (yea much stronger) Reasons I will prove, that* Presbyters *have Power to* Ordain.

Phil. Indeed your grofs Ignorance requires much Pity and Compaſſion. Don't you know that no Perfon may prefume to *Baptize,* unlefs he is a *lawful Minifter ?* For *Chrift* gave this *Commiſſion* only to his *Apoftles,* to their *lawful Succeſſors,* and to all others *Ordain'd* by them; and he join'd the Office of *Preaching* to it : So that *un-ordain'd* Perfons may as well prefume to *Preach* as to

Bap-

Baptize (*r*). And therefore the *Church* of old forbad *Women* to *Baptize*, and *Epiphanius* did account it ridiculous in *Marcion* and his Followers to permit *Women* to do this Office (*s*); and our *Church* requires it to be done by a *lawful Minister*. 'Tis certainly a moſt horrid Preſumption for a *Lay-man* to invade the *Miniſterial Office* without any *Commiſſion*; and as to the Pretence that an Infant may be in danger, I do verily believe the Infant may be as Safe upon the Stock of *God*'s Mercy without any *Baptiſm*, as with a *Baptiſm*, which is not commanded by *God*, and to which he has made no Promiſes. But the Reaſon why *Baptiſm* by *Laicks*, or by *Women*, ſuch as is moſt commonly practis'd in the *Roman Church*, is not eſteem'd *Null* by us, nor is repeated, is this; Be-

(*r*) *Petulantia autem Mulieris quæ uſurpavit docere, non etiam tingendi jus ſibi pariet.* Tert. de Bapt. cap. 17.
(*s*) *Epiphan. Panar. lib.* 1. *Tom.* 3. *hæreſ.* 42.

cauſe

caule we make a Difference between what is *Effential* to a *Sacrament,* and what is requifite in the Pe, lar way of ufing it. None cnd .. this among us, but thofe who queftion the whole *Chriftianity* the *Roman Church,* where the ƚ . *wives* do generally *Baptize:* But ii this invalidates the *Baptifm,* then we muft queftion all that is done among them: For Perfons fo *Baptized,* if their *Baptifm* is void, are neither truly *Ordain'd,* nor capable of any other *Act* of *Church-Communion.* Therefore Mens being in *Orders,* or their being duly *Ordain'd* is not neceffary to the *Effence* of the Sacrament of *Baptifm,* but only to the *Regularity* of its Adminiftration: And fo the want of it does not void it, but does prove fuch Men to be under great Defects and Diforders in their Conftitution. And agreeable to this was the Senfe of the *Ancient Chruch,* which did pofitively condemn the repeating of

Bap-

Baptifm (t), provided the Perfon was *Baptized in the Name of the Father, the Son, and the Holy Ghoft.* And when the Council of *Nice, Can.* 19. St. *Cyprian* and *Tertullian* fpeak of *Re-baptizing* thofe who had been *Baptiz'd* by *Hereticks*, it was becaufe they efteem'd their *Baptifm* void and null *(u)*, when not Adminiftred in the Name of the *Holy Trinity* according to our Bleffed *Saviour's* Appointment. So that *Baptifm* is no fit Prefcription for other *Clergy-Offices*, for the Effect does wholly depend on the *Sacrament*, that is, on the *Matter* and *Words* thereof rightly apply'd, not on the *Authority*, or *Power* of him who conferreth it; and fuch *Baptifm* is valid and unalterable, when done by any Perfon, tho' there was no neceffity for fuch an Adminiftration. Thus I have Invalidated your trifling Inftance, and have given you

(*t*) *Concil* 1. *Carthag.* **Can.** 1.*An.* 330. *item Concil.* 3. *Toletan.* (*u*) *Tertul. de Bapt. cap.* 15.

the

the true Senfe of the moft Learned Divines upon this Point, of which before (I find) you was utterly ignorant.

Pfeud. [*] *You are of a different Opinion from the old* Epifcopal Divines, *many of which were* Bifhops; *and tho' they judg'd* Ordination *by* Diocefans *to be moft Regular, and to tend to the* Bene effe, *the* Well-being *of the* Miniftry; *yet they did not fall into that Dotage, which has of late prevail'd among fome, to Dream, that it was neceffary to the* Effe *or very* Being *of the* Miniftry. *This I am fo well affur'd of, that I can (and will if it be needful) produce a Cloud of Witneffes from the* Writings *of thofe, that were unqueftionably* Epifcopal *in their* Judgment *and* Practice.

Phil. Thefe Divines, *Pfeudocheus,* whom you fpeak of, had one Heart for *Old England* and another for

New ; Thefe were the Men that by their lame and partial *Conformity* did very much contribute to the Growth of *Faction* fince the *Church's Reftauration*, for People have readily concluded, that certainly there muft be fomething that is very ill in our *Worſhip* and *Ceremonies*, otherwife fuch Men as were under the Obligations of *Oaths* and *Subfcriptions* would have fhew'd their Liking and Affent to them by a more regular *Conformity :* Thefe were a fort of Men that knew how to comply with weak and tender *Confciences*, tho' it was againft the Senfe of their own; Thefe could give the *Holy Sacrament* to any either ftanding or kneeling; Thefe could *Baptize* with the *Sign* of the *Crofs*, or without it; Thefe could vifit the Sick with the *Church's Prayers* or their own, as the Perfon was inclined; Thefe were the Men that have been always applauded by your *Party*, and by fuch you have ever

ex-

expected to compaſs your Deſigns;
and certainly there is no ſuch dangerous *Enemy*, as one within our own
Walls, that can betray us unſuſpected.
And tho' the like Men may acquire
from ſuch as you thoſe fine and cu-
rious Names of *Moderation, Diſcre-
tion* and *Prudence*, yet they will never ſerve the Intereſt of our *Holy
Religion*, or ſecure the *Honour* and
Safety of the *Engliſh Church*; For
when ſuch Perſons give Example and
Encouragement to others to break
the *Church's Laws*, and to contemn
her *Authority*; no wonder then, that
Vice and *Faction* does appear ſo *Inſo-
lent* and ſo *Daring*.

Pleud. *Pray*, Philalethes, *wave
that Topick, and let me hear how
you will prove that* Meer **Presbyters**
have no Power to admit into the Miniſtry *by* Impoſition of Hands *in*
Ordination.

Phil. I will prove it clearly from
the *Holy Scriptures*, which do not
afford one Inſtance, that *Meer Preſ-
byters*

byters did ever admit into the *Ministry* by *Impofition of Hands.* For the firft *Ordination* that we meet with in the *Holy Scriptures*, is that of thofe *Seven*, commonly call'd *Deacons*; And there we find no *Hands* impofed but thofe of the *Holy Apoftles.* *Act.* 6.

Pfeud. * *Hold,* Philalethes, *this Inftance of the Apoftles* Ordaining Deacons, *will not be fufficient to prove, that* Presbyters *may not* Ordain.

For, 1. *The* Apoftles *(as far as appears by the Context) were the only* Church-Officers *then prefent at* Jerufalem; *and therefore no wonder that the* Apoftles *only are mention'd to have* laid *on their Hands, when either they muft do it, or it could not then be done at all.*

2. *Tho' the* Apoftles *only* Ordain'd *the* Seven Deacons, *yet* Timothy *was* Ordain'd *by* Presbyters ‡, *as the*

* Mr. *J. W's Letters, p.* 15, 16. ‡ Pfeudocheus *contradicts himfelf, p.* 34.

Scri-

Scripture teſtifies, 1 Tim. 4.14. *From whence I argue thus* à Majore. *Thoſe that have* Power *to* Ordain *an* Evangeliſt, *(who is an* higher Officer*) have* Power *much more to* Ordain *a* Presbyter : *(who is an* inferior Officer) *But* Presbyters *have* Power *to* Ordain *an* Evangeliſt, *therefore they have* Power *to* Ordain Presbyters.

3. *The* Apoſtles *having* Ordain'd *the* Deacons *at* Jeruſalem, *is no Argument that none but* Apoſtles *may do this Work.* *For we Read in* Acts 13. 1, 2, 3. *That* Barnabas *and* Paul *receiv'd* Impoſition of Hands *from* Presbyters *without* Apoſtles. *The Words of the Text are theſe,* Now there were in the Church that was at *Antioch*, certain Prophets and Teachers, as *Barnabas* and *Simeon* ——as they miniſtred to the Lord and faſted, the Holy Ghoſt ſaid, Separate now unto me *Barnabas* and *Saul* for the work whereunto I have called them. And when they had faſted and prayed, and laid their
hands

hands on them, they sent them a-
way. *From whence it is apparent,
that those who* laid Hands *on* Barnabas *and* Paul, *were* Presbyters, *the
ordinary Pastors or Teachers of that*
Church, *which was at* Antioch. *So
that this is a sure Argument from
this Place, If* Presbyters *might* lay
their Hands *on* Apostles *themselves,
then they may* lay their Hands *on*
Presbyters *much more : But the* Antecedent *is true, therefore the* Con-
sequent.

    Phil. What strange Conjectures are
these, *Pseudocheus,* that have not
one *Text* to support them in all
the *Holy Scriptures?* You say, that
the *Holy Apostles* (as far as appears
by the Context) were the only
Church-Officers then present at *Jerusalem* ; and therefore no wonder,
that the *Apostles* are only mention'd
to have *laid* on their *Hands,* when
either they must do it, or it could
not be then done at all. 'Tis certainly
true, *Pseudocheus,* that the *Holy*
                      Apo-

Apoftles were the only *Church-Offi-cers* that had the *Power* of *Ordain-ing* the *Seven Deacons* ; for the *Se-venty Difciples* that were prefent at their *Ordination*, would not u-furp any *Authority* whereunto they were not *Commiffion'd* by the *Holy Jefus* ; and that *Commiffion* which they did receive, was not *Temporary*, and fuch as prefently expir'd, but was *Durable* and for Term of Life : For we find that when St. *Peter* ftood up in the midft of the *Difciples*, the Number of the Names (*i. e.* the Perfons) together were an Hundred and Twenty, and among thefe were the *Seventy* as well as the *Eleven*, *Acts* 1. 15. *(w)*. Again of the Number of thefe *Se-venty Difciples* were St. *Matthias* and St. *Barnabas* *(x)*, who ftood Competitors for the Apoftlefhip, from which *Judas* by Tranfgreffion

---

(*w*) *Vid. Lightf. in loc.* (*x*) *Eufeb. Hift. lib.* 1 *c.* 12. *& lib.* 2. *c.* 9. *Epiphan. Heref.* 20. *Hieron. de Script. Ecclef. in Matth. Vid. Irenæum lib.* 4. *c.* 63. *Tertul. de Præfcript.*

fell,

fell, and the Lot falling upon St. *Matthias*, he was chosen from the Inferior into the Superior *Order*, *Acts* 1. 26. Then also those *Jerusalem-Elders* (*i. e.* οἱ Πρεσβύτεροι *Priests*) so frequently mention'd in that first *General Council* there held (*y*) were no other than some of the *Seventy Disciples*, *Acts* 15. 2, 4, 6, 22. Now all these had no other *Commiſſion* than what they before receiv'd from our Bleſſed *Saviour*, of which they were still fully poſſeſs'd, and were present at the *Ordination* of the *Seven Deacons*, but had no Power to *Ordain* them.

2. You say, " *Tho' the* Holy Apo-
" ſtles *only* Ordain'd *the* Seven Dea-
" cons, *yet* Timothy *was* Ordain'd
" *by* Presbyters, *as the* Scripture te-
" ſtifies, 1 *Tim.* 4. 14." Who, but *Pseudocheus*, or such another, would ever have said so ? The *Scripture*

<hr>

(*y*) *Theſe are call'd* Presbyters *in the* Greek Originals, *which being often rendred* Seniores *in the* Vulgar Latin, *occaſion'd our firſt Tranſlators to call them* Elders.

testifies no such thing, it does not
say that he was *Ordain'd* by *Presbyters,* but by the *Presbytery* ; of
which St. *Paul* was the Chief, and
by the *Imposition* of his *Hands* (with
the *Hands* of other *Bishops*) was he
Ordain'd. As in 2 *Tim.* 1. 6. *Wherefore I put thee in remembrance, that
thou stir up the gift of God which is
in thee, by the putting on of my
Hands.* But that you may better
know the meaning of this Word
Presbytery, take this Information.
The Word Πρεσβυτέριον, *Presbytery,* is
only, us'd three times in the *New Testament* ; First in St. *Luke* 22. 66.
where we render it the *Elders* of
the People ; but it is in the *Original* the *Presbytery* of the People.
The second Place is in *Acts* 22.
5. where we read all the Estate
of the *Elders*, the Word is the
same, Πρεσβυτέριον, the whole *Presbytery.* Now the third Place is in
1 *Tim.* 4. 14. *Neglect not the Gift
that is in thee, which was given thee
by*

by Prophecy, with the Laying on of the Hands of the Presbytery. In the two firſt Places *Presbytery* is taken for the Magiſtrates or Senate of the People of the *Jews,* no *Chriſtian Order*; then from the uſe of the *Word* in other Places, it cannot be thought that this Place ſhould particularize this *lower Order,* as you fancy, ſince there is no Place to parallel it: But becauſe *Presbytery* doth ſignifie an *Eccleſiaſtical Order* in the *Miniſtry,* therefore this *Presbytery* ſhould do ſo likewiſe: but in as large a *Senſe* as *Presbyter,* and not in a more *reſtrain'd Senſe.* Now *Presbyter* takes in its *Latitude* the whole *Order* of *Prieſthood,* both *Biſhop* and *Presbyter:* So that this Place muſt be underſtood according to the Judgment of theſe Ancient Fathers, St. *Chryſoſtom, Theophylaƈt, Theodoret* and others, who ſaid that the *Presbytery* here mentioned, was not a *Presbytery* of the *Inferior Order,* but of that Rank of *Presbyters* which

which we term *Bishops* (*z*). Thus
I have prov'd that *Timothy* was not
Ordain'd by *Meer Presbyters*, and
shall next consider your Argument
à *Majore*, which is this. " Those
" that have Power to *Ordain* an
" *Evangelist*, (who is an higher
" Officer) have Power much more
" to *Ordain* a *Presbyter* : (who is
" an inferior Officer) But *Presby-*
" *ters* have Power to *Ordain* an
" *Evangelist* , Therefore they have
" Power to *Ordain Presbyters*."
Your *Minor* I deny, *Presbyters* never had any Power to *Ordain Evan-*
gelists, for they were Persons chosen
by the *Holy Apostles* to Preach the
Gospel to such as formerly had not
heard of it; at least, to such as had
yet resisted the Light of it, and were
not converted by it (*a*): Their
Rank in the *Church* was after the

(*z*) *The* Greek Fathers *and the* Ethiopick Version *do*
say that these were Bishops, *who join'd with St.* Paul *in ma-*
king Timothy *a* Bishop. 'Ου περὶ πρεσβυτέρων φησὶν ἐνταῦθα,
ἀλλὰ περὶ ἐπισκοπῶν Chrysost. & Theoph. in 1 Tim. 4. 14.
Impositione manuum Episcoporum. Vers. Æthiopic. (*a*) *Eu-*
seb. Hist. Eccles. *l.* 3 *c* 37.

D *Apo-*

Apostles and *Prophets*, and before the *Pastors* and *Teachers*. And he gave some, *Apostles:* and some *Prophets:* and some, *Evangelists:* and some *Pastors* and *Teachers: Eph.* 4. 11. (*b*) They differ'd from *Pastors* only in this, that those were *Stationary*, had a fix'd and settled Residence in *Churches* already planted; these were *Itinerant*, and went up and down to impart the *Holy Gospel*, according to their Instructions receiv'd from the *Apostles*; In short, their *Office* was twofold, to *Write*, as well as to *Preach*, which being Extraordinary, expir'd with the *Holy Apostles.* Here you see what an *Evangelist* was, but why *Timothy* is said to be only such, I cannot conceive; That *Text* in 2 *Tim.* 4. 5. will not prove him an *Evangelist*, and so does not support your drowning *Cause:* The Words are these Ἔργον ποίησον Ἐυαγγελιςɤ, *Do the* Work,

---

(*b*) *Some part of the Function of the first* Three *was Extraordinary and Temporary; In what was Ordinary and Perpetual Bishops do* Succeed,

not the Office *of an* Evangelist. And what's that? You may see it immediately going before, *verf.* 2. *Preach the Word, be instant in sea-son, out of season, reprove, rebuke, exhort with all long-suffering, and doctrine.* And if this be the *Work* of an *Evangelist*, which St. *Paul* would have *Timothy* to do, *viz.* To *Preach, to be instant in season, and out of season, &c.* 'tis certainly the *Work* of a *Bishop,* who ought to perform all this. But truly, *Pseudo-cheus,* I do very much wonder, that in your *levelling Humour* you did not reduce him to a *Deacon,* for the next Words that follow, are these, *ver.* 5. Τὴν Διακονίαν πληροφόρησον, *Fulfil thy Deaconship:* So that you might as well have call'd him a *Dea-con,* as an *Evangelist.*

But now your third Considerati-on, *Pseudocheus,* is wonderfully sur-prising. The *Apostles* (you say) having *Ordain'd* the *Deacons* at *Je-rusalem,* is no Argument that none but *Apostles* may do this Work. For

we

we read (you tell us) in *Acts* 13. 1, 2, 3. That *Barnabas* and *Paul* receiv'd *Imposition of Hands* from *Presbyters* without *Apostles*. The Words of the *Text* are these, *Now there were in the Church that was at* Antioch, *certain Prophets and Teachers, as* Barnabas, *and* Simeon *that was called* Niger, *&c.* (*c*) observe the Words, these are call'd *Prophets* and *Teachers*, and there is no mention of *Presbyters* in the whole Chapter; St. *Mark* the *Evangelist* was then present with them, but we do not find that he was any way concern'd in this *Imposition of Hands. Acts* 12. 25. *& Acts* 13. 5. These *Prophets* then were not such as *Agabus*, and the Daughters of *Philip* the *Evangelist*, but they were *Prophets* of extraordinary Prediction, next to *Apostles*, *Eph.* 4. 11. Such as *Epaphroditus*, and *Barna-*

(*c*) *These were common Maxims among the* Jews, Quicquid Prophetæ prædixerunt, possent facere, & Propheta omnia potest.

bas.

bas, and St. *Paul* himself (*d*). And although St. *Paul* had his *Immediate Call* by *Jesus Christ* (*e*), and St. *Barnabas* was one of the *Seventy Disciples* (*f*), yet it was by these *Prophets* at *Antioch* that they had their *Ordination* to the *Apostleship,* for before this they were not call'd *Apostles* (*g*), but are presently afterwards, *Acts* 14. 4, 14. This then was an *extraordinary Call,* and 'twas done by *extraordinary Means* and *Ministers,* not by *Presbyters,* as you shamefully assert, but by *Prophets,* even *Simeon, Lucius* and *Ma-*

(*d*) *Gal.* 19. Ἱ ταχθέντων ὑμῶν Ἀπόςολον, *Phil.* 2. 25. (*e*) *Gal.* 1. 1 *Acts* 9 (*f*) *St.* Barnabas *had no new Ordination from the* Holy Apostles, *when he Preach'd to the Christians at* Antioch, *Acts* 11. 23, 26. *for he did it by Virtue of that* Commission *he receiv'd from our Blessed* Saviour, *when he was made one of the* Seventy Disciples. (*g*) *Tho'* Simeon, Lucius *and* Manaen *did lay their Hands upon St.* Paul *and St.* Barnabas, *yet they receiv'd their* Ordination *to the* Apostleship, μᾶλλον δ᾽ ἀπὸ τῶ πνεύματ[ος], *rather by the* Holy Ghost : *And that they had not the* Apostleship *before, is manifest by what follow'd after, For we do not find in all the* Story *of their* Acts, *that either they* Ordain'd Presbyters, *or gave the* Holy Ghost, *or wrought any* Miracles, *which were the* Signs *of their* Apostleship, *before this* Solemn Ordination, *or* Imposition *of the* Hands *of the aforesaid three* Prophets ; *as afterwards we find they did in several Places of that* Book. Vid. Chrysostom. Hom. 20. in Act.

naen:

naen : Therefore in all this we may affirm with St. *Chryfoſtom,* ἔτας ἐδὲν ἀνθρώπων τὸν γενομέν, that of all the things which did befal St. *Paul* in his whole *Vocation,* there was nothing *Ordinary,* but every part was acted by the Hand of *God.* So that I deny this Argument which you draw from *Acts* 13. 1, 2, 3. *Presbyters* (ſay you) might *lay their Hands* on *Apoſtles* themſelves, therefore they may *lay their Hands* on *Presbyters* much more. Here your *Antecedent* is falſe, and therefore the *Conſequent :* For this *Power* of *Impoſition of Hands* in *Ordination* was fix'd upon the *Holy Apoſtles* and *Apoſtolick Men* (*b*), and was never communicated to the *Seventy Diſciples* or *Presbyters ;* for the *Apoſtles* and *Apoſtolick Men* did ſo *de Facto,* and were commanded ſo to do, and the *Seventy* and the *Presbyters* never did ſo ; therefore

(*b*) *They were* Prophets, *who are here call'd* Apoſtolick Men.

this

this *Office* of the *Apostleship* is di-
ſtinct, and Superior to that of *Pres-*
byters ; and this *Diſtinction* muſt be
ſo continu'd to all Ages of the *Chri-*
ſtian Church, for the thing was not
Temporary, but *productive of Iſſue*
and *Succeſſion* even to the end of
the World.

Pſeud. *Pray,* Philalethes, *which*
is the next Ordination *that you meet*
with in the Holy Scriptures ?

Phil. The next *Ordination, Pſeu-*
docheus, is that of *Presbyters* in
Act. 14. 23. and this was by St. *Paul*
and St. *Barnabas*, without the *Aſſi-*
ſtance of any *Presbyters* of thoſe
Times, or the *Suffrage* of the People.

Pſeud. * *Pray, Sir, permit me to*
give you my Explication of that Text.
The Word which we render there
[Ordain'd] *is in the Original Greek*
Χειςοτονησαντες, *which primarily ſignifies*
Suffragiis creare, *or to chooſe by*
Votes ; *which was* **uſually** *done by*

---

* Mr. *J. W*'s *Letters*, p 17.

ſtretch-

ftretching out of the Hand, *and is*
the Action *of the People. Whereas*
the Action *of the* Ordainers *is call'd*
Χ ε-Σεσία, *or* laying on of the Hands.
However, *I* grant, *that the* Impofition *of the* Apoftles Hands *concurr'd*
with the Peoples Choice, *in* Ordaining *thofe* Elders *in every* Church
mention'd in the Text.

Phil. If you had a little more convers'd with the *Criticks, Sir,* you
vould have found that Χειροτονήσαντες,
which in *Act.* 14. 23. is tranflated
Ordain'd, is a Phrafe of Speech,
Αττικῶς borrow'd from an Ancient
Greek Cuftom of *ftretching forth the*
Hand in a *Voting of Bufineffes,* and
'tis apply'd to God himfelf touching
his *fore-eternal* Choice of the *Apo-*
ftles to be Witneffes of the *Holy Gof-*
pel, Act. 10. 41. where it cannot
poffibly be taken in its *native Senfe,*
as it denotes a *choofing by Suffrage,*
no more than Συγκαταψηφίσθη, in the E-
lection of St. *Matthias* by *Lot,* which
is rendred, *he was numbred with*
the

the Eleven Apoftles, Act. 1. 26. For among the *Heathen*, their *Priefts* and *Magiftrates* were eligible by *Lots* (1), as well as by *Voices*, the *Priefts* efpecially, faith *Ariftotle, Pol. l.* 4. *c.* 15. This Word then does not fimply fignifie an *Impofition* or *Laying on of Hands*; for that the *Holy Ghoft* commonly expreffeth in other Terms, as Χειροθεσία, Επίθεσις των Χειρων, *Act.* 6. 6. 1 *Tim.* 4. 14. 2 *Tim.* 1. 6. But it befpeaks the whole compound Act confifting of both *Election* and *Ordination* together; and is the fame with Καταστήσης, *Tit.* 1. 5. generally to *Order* or *Appoint*, whether by *Suffrage* or without, and fo 'tis frequently us'd in *Claffic* Authors, (even Coëtaneous with St. *Luke*, or before him,) as Learned Mr. *Selden* has by moft *pregnant Inftances* at large prov'd it to my Hand, *De Synedr. l.* 1. *c.* 14. Now

(1) *Herodot. l.* 3. *c.* 83. *Demofth. contra Neær. Æfch. in Orat. contra Ctefiphont. Tacit. Annal, l.* 1. *c.* 11. *l.* 13 *c.* 6. &c.

this

this is an Act that is all along in *Scripture* solely afcrib'd to the chief *Governours* of the *Church*, as in the aforefaid Text, *Act.* 14. 23. will very eafily appear, if we confider but the *Context,* or *Grammatical Syntaxis* of the Words; *And when they had Ordain'd them Elders,* &c. what they? *They who came from* Derbe, *v.* 20. *Return'd thence to* Lyftra, Iconium *and* Antioch, *v.* 21. And thefe were none other than St. *Paul* and St. *Barnabas.* So that here is no Mention, or the leaft Intimation of the Peoples *joint Concurrence* in the *Action.* And truly I do not find in all the *Holy Scripture* any Footfteps of either *Right* or *Fact* as to *Popular Elections.* " For after our " Blessed *Saviour* did enter upon his " *Miniftry,* (faith Dr. *Comber*ᵀ) he " chofe his *Apoftles* and the *Seventy* " *Difciples* himfelf; and 'tis plain " he gave his *Apoftles* power to

---

* Dr. *Comber,* Vol. 2. *p.* 207.

chufe

" chufe and *Ordain* others, and left
" no manner of Intimation, that
" the People fhould have any
" fort of *Right* herein.   Then thofe
" Hundred and Twenty, who ap-
" pointed two *Candidates* for the
" vacant Place of *Judas*, and left
" the Choice, by *Lot* to God (*k*),
" were not all the *Believers*, but
" the *Apoftolical College* of *Paftors*
" (*l*), which confifted of the *Apo-*
" *ftles* and *Seventy Difciples*, and
" about thirty eight more of the
" principal *Difciples* fitted for the
" *Miniftries* of the *Church*, as a ve-
" ry Learned Divine hath prov'd
" (*m*). 'Twas the *Holy Ghoft* that
" chofe St. *Paul* and St. *Barnabas*
" (*n*).   And by the fame *Spirit*
" were the *Apoftles* only guided in
" choofing *Bifhops* for their fixed
" *Succeffors* (*o*), they had a pecu-

(*k*) *Solent, quæ forte dantur, dici divinitus dari.* Aug.
Gen. ad lit. l. 1. c. 18. (*l*) *Act.* 1. 23, 26. (*m*) Di.*Light-*
*foot's Works, Tom.*1. p. 744. *&c. & p.* 778. (*n*) *Act.* 13.
1, 2, 3.   (*o*) I *Tim.* 1. 18. *vid. Patr. citat. à Grot.*
in loc.

" liar

" liar *Gift* of discerning Spirits,
" and I new who were fittest for
" such *Offices* (*p*); they gave
" Rules to the *Bishops*, *Timothy* and
" *Titus*, what fort of Persons they
" should choose into the *Ministry*
" (*q*), therefore they then only
" had a *Right* to *Elect*. The Peo-
" ples part (observed by St. *Paul*)
" being no more but only to de-
" clare them blameless, as *Witnesses*
" of their *Conversation·* And cer-
" tainly so long as the *Holy Apo-*
" *stles* liv'd, who had such an *ex-*
" *traordinary Inspiration*; it had
" been the *highest Presumption* for
" the People to meddle any further
" in *Elections* than to applaud their
" *Choice.*Thus you see 'twas the *Spirit*
of *God* in those Times, which did de-
sign and mark out the Men, that
God intended to employ in his *holy*
Ministry. The Words of St. *Paul*

(*p*) 1 *Cor.* 12. 10. (*q*) *Vid. Theoph. Præf. ad* 1 *Ep. ad*
Tim. & ad Epist. ad Tit. See Act. 20. 28.——— *Over which*
the Holy Ghost hath made you Overseers, not the People.

to *Timothy* make this very clear,
where it is said, *Neglect not the Gift
that is in thee, which was given thee
by Prophesic,* &c. 1 *Tim.* 4. 14. and
that there went some *Prophesics* before concerning *Timothy,* you'll find
in 1 *Tim.* 1. 18. And St. *Chrysostom*
observes upon these Words, that in
those times ἀπὸ προφητείας ἐγίνετο ὁ ἱερεὺς,
the *Priests* and *Ministers* of *God*
were made by *Prophesic,* that is,
faith he, ἀπὸ τȣ πνεύματ@. ἁγίȣ, by the
Holy Ghost; and finally glossing on
these Words, he does thus express it ;
Ὁ Θεός σε ἐξελέξατο, *God,* faith he, did
elect thee to this weighty *Charge,* he
hath committed no small part of
his *Church* unto thee, ἐκ ἀνθρωπίνη γέγο-
νας ψήφȣ, no Mortal Man had any
hand in that *Designation*; and therefore take thou heed that thou difgrace not, nor dishonour so *divine*
a *Calling. Chrysost. Hom.* 5. *in* 1. *ad
Tim. c.* 1. The main Arguments for
Popular Elections, are some mista-
ken Passages of St. *Cyprian.* And tho'
this

this *Holy Father* fometimes did ufe to confult with the *Priefts, Deacons,* and *People* in *Ordaining* to the *lower Degrees,* yet the Reafon was this, that he might weigh every ones *Merits* and *Manners* by their *common Advice* (r): " But to fhew
" this gave them no *Right* to *Elect,*
" (faith Dr. *Comber* *) he there
" fpeaks of one that he *Ordain'd*
" privately, becaufe he knew the
" Perfon was *worthy* (s), and his
" next Epiftle prefents us with a
" like Cafe (t): Now it is not
" likely, this ftrict *Father* and *holy*
" *Martyr* would have chofen Men
" into his *Clergy,* without the *Peo-*
" *ple,* if they had a *Right* to *Elect.*
" 'Tis truly a great Wonder, that
" Men to gratifie a *Party,* fhould
" fuppofe that *Chrift,* or his
" *Apoftles* were the *Authors* of a
" thing fo naturally tending to di-

(r) *Solemus vos ante confulere, &c.* Cypr. Ep 33. p 76.
* Dr. *Comber,* Vol. 2. p 210. (s) *Cypr. ep. cad* p. 77.
(t) Cypr. ep. 34. p 80. *Vid. item ep* 35, p 84.

" vide

" vide and difgrace the *Church*, and
" fo manifeftly the caufe of *Confufion*
" and every *evil Work:* 'Tis well
" known the Generality of the Peo-
" ple are fuch *incompetent Judges*,
" that if they had fuch a *Right*, the
" moft *Votes* would commonly fall
" on the *worft Men* (*u*), an *empty*,
" *cunning* and *plaufible Hypocrite*
" would eafily get more *Suffrages*
" among the *Mob*, than the moft
" *knowing*, *humble* and *holy Men*,
" who leaft feek the *Honour* they
" moft deferve".

Pfeud. *You need not fay any more*
concerning Popular Elections; *nor*
will I trouble you any further at this
time about the Ordination *of* Timothy; *'tis true, I did fay that he*
was Ordain'd *by* Presbyters *, *but*
now, I confcfs, I am inclin'd to
think that he was Ordain'd *by the*
Hands *of the Apoftle* Paul, 2 *Tim.* 1.6.

(*u*) Φαῦλℭ κριτής παντὸς χαλᾶ πράγματℭ ὁ ὀχλℭ. Py-
thag. ap. Stobæum. * *See Letters concerning the* Ordinat-
on *by* Presbyters, *by J. W. p.* 18.

yet will not this at all help your Cause, *nor prove, that the* Ordination *perform'd by a* Presbytery *is insufficient.*

Phil. An *Ordination* that is perform'd by such a *Presbytery*, as is mention'd in 1 *Tim.* 4. 14. is truly sufficient, for the *Presbytery* there spoken of, as I told you before, was not a *Presbytery* of the *Inferior Order*, but of that Rank of *Presbyters* which we term *Bishops*. And 'tis certainly true, that the *Presbyters laying on of Hands* only, and always with a *Bishop*, cannot imply their having any direct *Power* in *Ordination*, but only their *Agreement* to the *Election*, testify'd by their *publick Concurrence* in this Act of their *Solemn Admission.*

Pseud. *Say you so, Sir? I desire then you would please to answer these Questions.*

1. *Whether a* Bishop *may delegate this* Power *of* laying on Hands *with him*

him in Ordination *to a* Lay-man, *or only to a* Presbyter [*]? *The first you will not say, I am confident; for you know what would follow from that Conceſſion. But if you say the Second,* viz. *That this* Power *can be delegated only to a* Presbyter, *then I ask again,*

2. *What Reaſon can be given why a* Presbyter *only may* lay *on Hands with the* Biſhop, *unleſs it be a Work belonging to his* Office, *as well as to the* Biſhop's? *For if it belong to him only by Virtue of a* Delegation *from the* Dioceſan; *then if a* Biſhop *give a* Delegation *to a* Lay-man, *to* lay on Hands *with himſelf, this will Authorize him as much as a* Presbyter.

Phil. 'Tis thought by many Learned Men, *Pſeudocheus,* that *John Calvin* would never have been a *Presbyterian,* if he had been better acquainted with *pious Antiquity,* and *Eccleſiaſtical Hiſtory;* whoſe Ig-

---

* Mr. *J. W*'s *Letters,* p 19.

E   norance

norance therein was much to be pitied, becaufe it led him into fuch unaccountable and extravagant Errors. And if you had ever read any thing of the *Government* of the *Primitive Church* or the *Decrees* of her *Councils*, you would never have propos'd thefe *idle, frivolous* and *impertinent Queftions:* Sure you know in the firft Place, That a *Bifhop* cannot delegate this *Power* of *laying on of Hands* with him in *Ordination* to a *Lay-man*, becaufe fuch Men are prohibited to act therein by all our *Laws*, as well *Humane*, as *Divine*. And in the Second Place, it may not be amifs to tell you; that altho' the fourth *Council* of *Carthage**, which was held in the Year 401. did *Decree*, That when a *Presbyter* was *Ordain'd*, the *Bifhop blefling* him, and holding his *Hand* upon his Head, *etiam omnes Presbyteri, qui præfentes funt, manus fuas jux-*

---

* *Concil. Carthag. 4. Can. 3.*

ta

ta manum Epifcopi fuper caput illi-us teneant; all the *Presbyters* which are prefent, fhall likewife *lay their Hands* upon his *Head,* near the *Hand* of the *Bifhop*, yet it is as true withal, that this *Conjunction* of the *Presbyters* in the *Solemnities* of this *Act,* was rather *ad Honorem Sacer-dotii quam Effentiam Operis,* more for the *Honour* of the *Prieſthood* than for the *Eſſence* of the *Work.* And if you do obferve, this *Canon* doth not fay, that if there be no *Presbyters* in place, the *Biſhop* fhould defer the *Ordination* till they came; but *Presbyteri qui præfentes funt,* if any *Presbyters* were prefent at the doing of it, they fhould *lay their Hands* upon his *Head,* near the *Hand* of the *Bifhop.* So that howe-ver the *Presbyters* did *impoſe Hands* with the *Biſhop,* upon the Perfon to be *Ordain'd,* and fo concurr'd in the performance of the *outward Ceremo-ny*; yet the whole *Power* of *Ordina-tion* was vefted in the *Perfon* of the

E 2 *Bi-*

Bishop only, as to the *Essence* of the
Work. And in the *Greek Church,*
none but the *Bishop lays on his Hand*
at the *Ordination* of a *Priest,* as well
as of a *Deacon* (s); for *Epiphanius*
faith, How can a *Presbyter Ordain,*
or *constitute* a *Presbyter,* μὴ ἔχων Χι-
εϛοτ̓σίαν τῆ χειροτονίᾳ, who in his *Ordination* did receive no *Power* to *impose Hands* upon another (t) ?
Thus 'tis plainly evident that *Meer
Presbyters* have no *Power* to *Ordain*
into the *Ministry* by *Imposition of
Hands,* that all such *Ordinations* have
been ever accounted as *Nullities,* and
consequently that the *Dissenting
Teachers,* who have been only *Ordain'd* by their *Rebel-Priests,* are
not qualify'd to perform any *Mini-
sterial Acts,* without a *new* and *lawful Ordination.* But for your farther Satisfaction, *Pseudocheus,* in
several of the foregoing Matters, I
would advise you to consult St. *Paul's*

(s) *Euchol. in Ordin. Diac.* p. 250. & *in Ordin. Presbyt*
p. 293. (t) *Epiphan. Haeres.* 75. *contra Aerium.*

Epi-

Epistles to *Timothy* and *Titus*, in
which we have the exact *Platform* of
the *Church's Ministry*, as communicated and perpetuated from the *Holy
Apostles.* ˹ Observe then the *Church*
of *Ephesus*, and the *Churches* of
Crete. In them we find many *Presbyters*, and above those *Presbyters*
in *Dignity* and *Office Timothy* and
Titus.

Pseud. ˹ *I have thoroughly consulted the Epistles to* Timothy *and* Titus, *Yet cannot find therein any* Plat-
form *of* Diocesan Prelacy, *nor the
least Word in favour of it.* I have
observ'd also in the Church of Ephesus *many* Presbyters; *which* Presbyters *were the same with* Bishops *both
in* Name *and* Office : *For so the* Scripture *it self tells me*, Acts 20. 17.
And from *Miletus* he sent to *Ephesus*, and called for the Elders [τὺς
Πρεσβυτέρυς] or Presbyters] *of the*
Church. *Compare this with v.* 28.

---

* *Bp. Mossom* on *Matth.* 28. 19, &c. * Mr. *J. W's Letters, p.* 20.

Take

Take heed therefore unto your felves and to all the Flock, over which the Holy Ghoft hath made you Overfeers, [Ἐπισκόπους, Biſhops] to Feed [*or* Guide *and* Rule , ποιμαίνειν] the Church of God——*The fame Perfons whom the* Apoftle *calls* Elders *in v. 17. He calls* Biſhops *in v. 28. and charges it upon them as their* Duty, (*effential to their* Office) *to* Rule *as well as to* Teach *the* Church *committed to their* Charge.

Phil. When a *Schifmatick* has ftifled the *Convictions* of his *Confcience*, and fettl'd his *Felicity* upon *worldly Advantages*; then he is perverfly *Blind* to the *brighteft Truths*, that *thwart* and *oppofe* his *Schifmatical Principles:* He cannot difcern the exact *Platform* of the *Church's Miniftry* in the Epiftles to *Timothy* and *Titus*, becaufe 'tis fo deftructive to his *upftart* and *novel Devices.* Now in thefe Epiftles are moft *excellent Inftructions*, how a *Biſhop* ought to behave himfelf in fuch a *weighty Office,*

Office, and 'twas very convenient and neceſſary, that theſe ſhould be recorded at the firſt *Inſtitution* of *Epiſcopacy*, and *Settlement* of the *Church* in that Courſe, wherein it was to continue, being deſtitute of the *extraordinary Aſſiſtance* of the *Holy Apoſtles.* And in theſe is alſo manifeſted the *Power*, as well as the *Duty* of a *Biſhop.* Which is,

1ſt. To take Care that no *Innovation* in *Doctrine* be admitted, and to *puniſh* all *Heretical* and *Schiſmatical Teachers*, which tranſgreſs'd his *Commands*, as St. *Paul* ſays, *he had excommunicated and delivered over to Satan*, Hymeneus *and* Alexander, 1 *Tim.* i. 3, 20.

2dly. To order the *Publick Aſſemblies* both as to *Prayers* and *Teaching*, 1 *Tim. chap.* 2.

3dly. To *Ordain* the *Clergy* or *Church-Officers*, both ſuch as were to ſupply *vacant Places*, and to *ſucceed* him, and them alſo, with their ſeveral *Qualifications*, 1 *Tim. ch.* 3.

4thly.

4thly. To teach himfelf, and command others to teach *found Doctrine*, and to refufe or reject all *Novelties* either in *Doctrine* or *Practice*. Where St. *Paul* gives warning with what *Herefies* he muft expect to be troubled, 1 *Tim. ch.* 4. *v.* 11. and how he ought to demean and behave himfelf in his own particular *Converfation* and *Affairs*.

5thly. To execute *Ecclefiaftical Jurifdiction* over the whole *Church*, and to be wary in his *Ordinations*, 1 *Tim. ch.* 5. 21, 22. and to fee that all forts of Perfons perform their *Duties* as they ought to do. And in the Second Epiftle you will find feveral *Injunctions* and *Exhortations* of the fame Nature with thofe in the Firft.

Then afterwards St. *Paul* in his Epiftle to *Titus*, whom he had made *Bifhop* of *Crete*, does charge him to fet in Order the things that were wanting, and to *Ordain Elders* in every City (*u*). Several of the

(*u*) *Tit.* 1. 5, 9, 13.

Cha-

Characters, by which he was to try them, are alfo fet down; He is charged to rebuke the People *fharply*, and to fpeak the things that became *found Doctrine*; He is inftructed concerning the *Doctrines* he was to teach, and thofe he was to avoid; and alfo how to *cenfure* an *Heretick*: He was to admonifh him twice, and if that did not prevail, he was to reject him by fome *publick Cenfure* (w). Now thefe *Admonitions* had been to no manner of purpofe, if *Timothy* and *Titus* had not a *Power* of *Ordaining Presbyters*, and a *Jurifdiction* over them. It is certain there were *Elders* in the *Church* of *Ephefus*, before *Timothy* was left there (x), and probably in *Crete*, before *Titus* was fettled in that place, for it was St. *Paul's* Cuftom to Ordain *Presbyters* in every *Church* (y): And if thefe *Presbyters* could have *Ordain'd* others as the number of

---

(w) *Tit.* 3. 10, (x) *Act.* 20. 17. (y) *Act.* 14. 23

Con-

Converts increas'd, it would certainly have been very needless to set any
Persons over them to perform that
Office. And that *Timothy* and *Titus*
had not this *Power* committed to
them as *Evangelists*, is most certain,
because *Evangelists*, as such, had not
that *Power :* For then *Meer Deacons*
might have *Ordain'd* and *Govern'd
Priests*, for such was *Philip* the *E-
vangelist*, yet he never attempted to
do it (*z*). But you further say,
that you have observ'd in the *Church*
of *Ephesus* many *Presbyters* ; and
that those *Presbyters* were the same
with *Bishops* both in *Name* and *Office:*
Then you tell me, the *Scriptures*
inform you so, *Act.* 20. 17. *And
from* Miletus *he sent to* Ephesus, *and
called for the Elders* [τὰς Πρεσβυτέρας]
or Presbyters of the Church. And
then you say, compare this with
v. 28. *Take heed therefore unto your
selves and to all the Flock, over*

(*z*) *Compare Act.* 21. 8. *with Act.* 6. 5.

which

which the Holy Ghoſt hath made you Overſeers, [Ἐπισκόπες, *Biſhops*] *to Feed* [or Guide and Rule, ποιμαίνειν] *the Church of God*—— So that the ſame Perſons whom the *Apoſtle* calls *Elders* in the 17th *verſ.* you ſay, he calls them *Biſhops* in the 28th *verſ.* Now what is this, *Pſeudocheus*, but a *wreſling* of the *Holy Scriptures* from their true *Senſe* and *Meaning* to ſerve your own *Purpoſes* and *Deſigns?* For theſe were not all *Meer Presbyters* that heard this *Farewel Sermon* of St. *Paul*, but here were ſeveral *Biſhops* alſo, and this is teſtified by a *Witneſs* beyond all exception, even the Ancient St. *Irenæus*, whoſe *Integrity* and *Authority* no *Presbyterian* did ever dare to diſpute ; He liv'd within 180 Years of the Birth of *Chriſt*, and was the *Diſciple* of St. *Polycarp*, who was brought up at the Feet of St. *John* the *Apoſtle*, and convers'd with many *Apoſtolick Men*. His Words are theſe, *In Mileto enim convocatis Epiſcopis*

scopis & Presbyteris, qui erant ab Epheso, & a reliquis proximis Civitatibus, quoniam ipse festinaret Hierosolymis Pentecosten agere, &c. *(a)* St. *Paul* making haft to keep his *Pentecost* at *Jerusalem,* at *Miletus* did call together the *Bishops* and *Presbyters,* from *Ephesus,* and the Neighbouring Cities. Now to all these did St. *Paul* speak, and to these the *Holy Ghost* had committed his *Church* to be fed and taught with *Pastoral Inspection,* but in the mean time here is no *Commission* of *Power,* or *Jurisdiction,* that was given to *Presbyters* distinctly, nor any supposition of such *præ-existent Power.*
" But to put this Matter out of all
" farther doubt, faith *Bp. Taylor* *,
" we have all the reason imagina-
" ble to believe, that many of these
" *Presbyters,* which came from *E-*
" *phesus* and the other Parts of

(*a*) I. *en. lib.* 3. *cap.* 14. * *Episcopacy asserted,* pag 14, 16.

" *Asia*

" *Afia the lefs* *, were made *Bifhops*
" at *Miletus*, for it was agreeable
" to the Practife of the *Holy Apo-*
" *ftles*, and the exigence of the
" thing it felf, that when they were
" to leave a *Church*, they then did
" fix a *Bifhop* in it, for why elfe
" was a *Bifhop* plac'd in *Jerufalem*,
" fo long before there were any in
" other *Churches*, but becaufe the
" *Apoftles* were to be difpers'd from
" thence, and there the firft *bloody*
" *Field* of *Martyrdom* was to be
" fought. And the Cafe was equal
" here, for St. *Paul* was never to
" fee the *Churches* of *Afia* any
" more, and he forefaw, that *ra-*
" *vening Wolves* would enter into
" the *Folds*, and he had actually
" fix'd a *Bifhop* in *Ephefus*, and
" 'tis unimaginable, that he would
" not make equal Provifion for o-
" ther *Churches*, there being the

---

* *The* Proconfular Afia, *or* Afia the lefs, *comprehended only* Ionia *and* Æolis, *with the Iflands of the* Ægean Sea, *and about the* Hellefpont.

fame

" fame neceffity from the fame dan
" ger, in them all, and either St.
" *Paul* did it now or never; for in
" *ver.* 25. he tells them, *And now,*
" *behold,* **I** *know that ye all, among*
" *whom* **I** *have gone preaching the*
" *Kingdom of God, fhall fee my Face*
" *no more.* And 'tis very plain that
" about this time, the other fix *Afi-*
" *an Churches* had *Angels* or *Bifhops*
" fet in their *Candlefticks*; for there
" had been a *Succeffion* in the *Church*
" at *Pergamus,* *Antipas* was dead;
" and *Timothy* had fat in *Ephefus,*
" and St. *Polycarp* at *Smyrna* many
" Years before St. *John* did write his
" *Revelation.*

Pfeud. * *But hold, Sir, I find the*
fame thing in the Churches *of* Crete,
which I before obferv'd in the Church
of Ephefus, *that thofe Perfons whom
the* Apoftle *calls* Elders, *he alfo calls*
Bifhops, *who were the very fame
with* Presbyters *both in* Name *and*

_____
† Mr. *J. W*'s *Letters,* p. 20.

Office,

Office, Tim. 1. 5, 6, 7. *compar'd to-gether* ; For this caufe left I thee in *Crete*, that thou fhouldeft fet in order the things that are wanting, and ordain Elders in every City, as I had appointed thee. If any be blamelefs ——*For a* Bifhop *muft be blamelefs*, &c.

Phil. What makes you fpeak of *Tim.* 1. 5, 6, 7? I fuppofe you mean *Tit.* 1. 5, 6, 7. And to what purpofe do you produce thefe *Texts?* Do you fancy the *Elders* here to be *Ordain'd*, were to be no other than *Meer Presbyters?* If fo, I muft rectifie your wrong Notions of them by a true Expofition of thofe *Verfes.* As foon as St. *Paul* had *Ordain'd Titus Bifhop* of *Crete*, his firft Work was τὰ λείποντα ἐπιδιορθώσαι, to fet in Order the things that were wanting, *viz.* to conftitute *Rites* and *Forms of publick Liturgy*, to erect a *Confiftory* for cognizance of *Criminal Caufes*, to dedicate *Houfes* for *Prayer*, and other *Divine Services*, and in a word,
by

by his *Authority* to establish such *Discipline* and *Rituals*, as himself did judge might be most suitable for the *Edification* and *Ornament* of the *Church* of God. For he that was appointed by St *Paul* to set things in Order, to supply what was defective, and to correct what was amiss, was most certainly thought by him to be the fittest Judge of a'l those *Obliquities* which he was to rectifie.

Then in the next Place, he was to *Ordain Elders* (that is *Presbyters)* in every City. Not *Presbyters* collectively in every City, but distributively, καλὰ πόλιν, City by City, that is, *Presbyters* in several Cities, one in a City. Now these *Elders* or *Presbyters* were very *Bishops*, one of which was appointed for every City, and the *Suburbicarian Region* thereof. And this is most agreeable not only to the Exposition of the *Ancient Church*, (the best *Comment*, when all is done, upon doubtful Places

Places of *Holy Scripture*,) but to
the *Text* it felf; and the Diftribution of thefe *Presbyters* by *Cities*, the
peculiar *Seats* of *Bifhops*, is according to the *Scheme* of *Ancient Church*
and the *Method* which the *Bleffed
Apoflles* thought good to ufe in the
planting and *modeling* of it. Then
fee how all this is confirm'd by the
Context, which exprefly calls them
Bifhops in *ver.* 7. Now were it not
for this, and what follows afterwards, we might be perhaps at liberty to leave the *Word* at large in
its *general Acception*, as it takes in
both *Orders*, both ufeful in every
City, and fo both to be fupply'd by
Titus: But we are fully convinc'd in
this *Matter*, for tho' Πρεσβύτερ⊙ in
the *New Teſtament* doth fometimes
fignifie a *Bifhop*, and fometimes a
Presbyter; yet that Ἐπίσκοπ⊙ doth
always fignifie a *Bifhop*, I fhall not
doubt to affirm. Becaufe it cannot
be fhewed in all the *Holy Scriptures*
that any *Meer Presbyter* is called a
F *Bifhop*

Bishop, but it may be often found that a *Bishop*, nay, an *Apostle* is called a *Presbyter*, for St. *Peter* entitles himself a *Co Presbyter*, 1 *Pet.* 5. 1. St. *John* calls himself a *Presbyter*, 2 *Joh.* 1. 3 *Joh.* 1. And St. *Paul* calls himself frequently Διάκονۛ, a *Deacon*, *Col.* 1. 23, 25. 1 *Cor.* 3. 5. 2 *Cor.* 3.6. 2 *Cor.* 6. 4.   'Tis the Observation of St. *Chrysostom* (in *Philip*) ᾗ, διάκονۛ ἐπίσκοπۛ ἐλέγετο, διὰ τᾶτο γράφων τῶ Τιμοθέῳ ἔλεγε, τίω Διακονίαν σε πληροφόρησον, Ἐπισκόπῳ ἂπι.   And a *Bishop* was call'd a *Deacon*, wherefore writing to *Timothy* he saith to him being a *Bishop*, *Fulfil thy Deaconship**.   And truly ever since that St *Peter* did set us an Example in the *Compellation* of the *Prototype*, calling him the *great Shepherd* and *Bishop* of our Souls, 1 *Pet.*

---

* *See Phil chap. 1. ver. 1.* ———— *with the Bishops and Deacons. Now these* Bishops *were not* Bishops *of* Philippi *that one City, but the* Bishops *of several neighbouring Cities in* Macedonia, *who did Assemble At* Philippi, *when* Epaphroditus *the* Bishop *thereof was at* Rome, *and then did receive St.* Paul's Epistle, *which was directed to the* Philippians. *And then under the Word* Deacons, *i.e.* Ministers, *both* Presbyters *and* Deacons *were comprehended.*

2. 25. and *St. Paul* also in calling
him an *Apostle Heb.* 3. .. and a
Deacon or *Minister, Rom.* 15. 8.
there is no *Word or Defignation* of a-
ny *Clerical Office*, but it has been given to *Bishops* and *Apostles*.

Pfeud. *I cannot fee, Philalethes,
that thefe Obfervations are true,
which you make concerning* Timothy
and Titus, *unlefs I had your* Spectacles; *but I do difcern that they were
in* Dignity *and* Office *above* Presbyters, *becaufe they were* Evangelifts.

Phil. Τί τυφλῷ ἢ κατόπτρῳ. What has
Pfeudocheus to do with *Spectacles?*
I wifh you could be fenfible, how
wonderfully you are involv'd in
Darknefs, in fuch a *Darknefs*, that
is *Ignorantia Veritatis*, an *Ignorance*
of *divine Truth*, even a *mental Dim-
nefs* and *Obfcurity* in refpect of God
and things *Divine*. So that in
whomfoever fuch *Ignorance* dwel-
leth, there is no *Light* at all, but

---

* Mr. *J. W's Letters*, p. 26.

Dark-

Darkness hangs like a *thick Fog* a-
bout them.   1*st. Darkness in the
Eyes*, *Pfal.* 69. 23.   Then 2*dly. Darkness in the Heart*, *Rom.* 1. 21.   And
3*dly. Darkness in the Underftand-
ing too*, *Eph.* 4. 18.   And why this
threefold Darkness ? Becaufe they
are *alienated* from the *Life* of *God*,
thro' the *Ignorance* that is in them,
and all this from the *Blindness* of
their *Heart*.   Therefore, *Pfeudocheus*, in compaflion to your many *In-
firmities*, I cannot choofe but inform
you thus much ; That there is not
one among all the *Ancient Fathers*,
that makes *Timothy* or *Titus Evangelifts* by *Office*:   But I find St. *Chryfoftom* (upon E*phef.* 4.) perempto-
rily faying, that neither *Timothy* nor
Titus were *Evangelifts* ; and there is
not any Perfon, no not *Calvin*, nor
Beza, that ever made it a part of an
Evangelifts Office, either to give *Orders*, or the *Power* of *Jurifdiction*.
For an *Evangelift* is, as I told you
before, no other than a *Writer* or
Preacher

Preacher of the *Holy Gospel*; so
that to do the *Work* of an *Evangelist*,
is no more, but to *Preach* the *Holy
Gospel:* 'Tis true many of them did
Travel, but they were never the more
Evangelists for that, for the *Office*
of an *Evangelist* does not imply a
perpetual Motion. Indeed, Sir, to
deal a little freely with you, 'tis really my Opinion, that you cannot
believe these *unaccountable Whimsies,*
which you endeavour to obtrude upon the World, but you think this
way to drive on your *Designs* with
the People, who hearing the Name
of an *Evangelist,* and not knowing
what it is, imagine any thing of it
what you please to insinuate ; as that
an *Evangelist* had some *transcendent
Power* over *Presbyters,* both to *Ordain,* and to *Govern* them, which
was not *communicable* to others ; but
you never shew that any such *Authority* was ever assign'd to them, or a-
ny such *Duty* ever exacted from
them. Now all these things being
rightly consider'd, 'tis very evident

that'

that both *Timothy* and *Titus* had E-
piscopal *Jurisdiction,* if not something more; and that this Name of
Evangelist, which you impose upon
them, is for no other end and purpose but *meer Trick* and *Delusion.*

Plend. *Pray what do you mean,
when you say, that* Timothy *and* Titus *had Episcopal Jurisdiction, if
not something more?*

Lord. All the *Ancients* do say that
Timothy and *Titus* had greater *Jurisdiction* than the *ordinary Episcopal:* (1) either of *Secondary Apo-*

---

(1) *Vide Fragment of* Polycrates *concerning the Martyrdom of* Timothy, *in* Photii Bibliothec. n 254 *in which
he saith,* ὅτι ὁ ἱερὸς Τιμόθεος ὑπὸ τῶ μεγάλε
Παύλε χειροτονηθεὶς τῆς τῶν Ἐφεσίων μετροπόλεως Ἐπίσκοπος, καὶ ἐν-
θρονισθεὶς, *that the Apostle* Timothy *was both* Ordain'd Bishop of the Metropolis of Ephesus, *and also there* Inthron'd.
Now this Polycrates *was* Bishop of the Church of Ephesus,
and was born within six or seven and thirty Years after St.
John *wrote unto the Angel of that Church, as appears by that*
Epistle, *which he sent unto* Victor Bishop of Rome, *wherein*
he saith, ἑπτὰ μὲν ἦσαν συγγενεῖς μου ἐπίσκοποι, ἐγὼ δὲ ὄγδοος,
that Seven of his Kinsmen were Bishops, *himself being the*
Eighth Polycrat. *Epist. ad* Victorem: apud Euseb. l. 5.
Hist. Eccl. cap. 24. *And we had it openly declar'd in the*
General Council of Chalcedon, *by* Leontius Bishop of Mag-
nesia, *that* ἀπὸ τῆς ὅσιης Τιμοθέε μέχρι νῦν. &c. *there had been*
a continued Succession of 27 *Bishops of the Church of Ephesus, from Holy* Timothy *unto his Time.* Concil. Chal. Act.
11. vid. Chrys. Hom. 1. in Tit. Hier. de Script. Eccles.
Ambros. in praefat. ad Tim. cap. 3. Primas. in 1 Tim. Greg.
de Cur. Past. par. 2. cap. 11,

stles

ſtles, as *Theodoret* and others, or
(as many ſay) *Archiepiſcopal.* For
to *Timothy* was committed all *Aſia
the leſs,* in which were many *Biſhops*
fix'd there by the *Holy Apoſtles:*
And *Titus* had the Charge over the
whole Iſle of *Crete,* in which there
were many *Biſhops* beſides [*].

Pſeud. † *If what* Theodoret *and
others do report be true, then* Timothy *and* Titus *were not* Biſhops (*pro-
perly ſpeaking*) *but* Archbiſhops,
having Biſhops *under them; and con-
ſequently, that* Ordination *was* not
peculiar to themſelves. For Ordination *belongs to* Biſhops, *as ſuch, according to your own Principles. And
thus you would be guilty of a* Self-
Contradiction.

Phil. I am not guilty of any *Self-
Contradiction,* Sir, but you are guilty here of a moſt *notorious Blunder;
ſed Riſum teneatis Amici!* Methinks
you ſhould have known, that *Arch-*

---

[*] *Vid. Miræi lib.* 4 *de Not. Epiſc. p.* 181. † Mr. *J. W's
Letters, p.* 23.

bi-

bishops and *Bishops* are the same in *Order*, tho' different in *Jurisdiction*: And that every *Archbishop* has his peculiar *Diocese*, as well as his *Province*, in which *Diocese* he has the sole *Power* of conferring *Orders*. So that an *Archbishop* is no other than the *highest* of the *Bishops*, who is as a *Head* set over other *Bishops*: And altho' we do not meet with this *Word* in the *Holy Scriptures*, yet it agrees thereunto for the preserving of *Order* in the *Church*; therefore 'tis prudent and useful to constitute *Degrees* in the *Church* of different *Dignity* and *Authority*. In the *Old Testament*, there was a *High-Priest*, and *Priests* of a second and inferior *Order*: In the *New*, there were *Apostles*, *Prophets*, *Evangelists*, *Pastors* and *Teachers*: And it is not contrary to the *Word of God*, that one should be above another in the *Church* for *Governments* sake.

Pseud. *Well, but the* Scripture *does not give the least Ground to think,* that

that *** Timothy *and* Titus *were Jettled, the one over* Asia the lefs, *the other over* Crete; *as* Bifhops *or* Metropolitans, *any more than over other Places, where they came; but plainly the contrary, as* Mr. Prynne *has unanfwerably made appear in his Book of the* Unbifhoping of Timothy and Titus, *pag.* 37. *and* 72. *He proves from* Scripture *their feveral Removes from Place to Place, which fhews them to be no fettled* Bifhops *or* Archbifhops, *but* Evangelifts *and* Itinerant Preachers. *Therefore* Theodoret *and others affirming the contrary, is no Argument againft* Scripture-Teftimony.

Phil. What a *wretched* and *perverfe Age* do we live in, when the *falfe* and *frivolous Stories of Infamous* Prynne fhall procure more *Faith* and *Credit* with a ftrange fort of *People,* than all the *Authorities* and *Teftimonies* of the *pious, primi-*

ſ *** Mr. *J. W's Letters,* p. 23.

tive

tive *Bishops* and *ancient Fathers* of our *Church!* All which do unanimously affert, That *Timothy* was *Bishop* of *Ephefus*, and that *Titus* was *Bishop* of *Crete*. I know very well that *Prynne* and fome others of your *Party* do raife feveral trifling *Objections* against *Timothy*'s being a *Pattern* for *Epifcopal Power*; for, they fay, "That St. *Paul* did fend him
" up and down to feveral Places, as
" he thought fit. He took him firft
" of all into his Attendance at *Ly-*
" *ftra* (*c*); from whence he accom-
" pany'd him thro' *Phrygia*, *Gala-*
" *tia*, *Macedonia* (*d*), and thefe
" from *Philippi* to *Theffalonica* and
" *Berea* (*e*). And when he went
" to *Athens*, he fent for *Timo-*
" *thy* to him (*f*), and fent him
" back from thence to *Theffalonica*;
" and he return'd from *Macedonia*
" (*g*) to him at *Corinth* (*h*).

(*c*) *Act.* 16. 3. (*d*) *Act.* 16. 6, 12. (*e*) *Act.* 17. 1, 10. (*f*) *Act.* 17. 15. (*g*) 1 *Theff.* 3. 1, 2. (*h*) *Act.* 18 5.

" From

" From thence St. *Paul* went into
" *Syria* (*i*), and fo to *Ephefus* (*k*);
" and there again he fent *Timothy*
" into *Macedonia* with *Eraftus* (*l*);
" whither St. *Paul* went afterwards
" himfelf (*m*). And upon his re-
" turn to *Miletus*, he fpeaks to the
" *Elders*, and not to *Timothy* as
" their *Bifhop*. From hence, they
" fay, St. *Paul* took him to *Jerufa-*
" *lem*, and fo to *Rome*, as appears
" by the *Epiftles* written from
" thence". " Now from this *Se-*
" *ries* of the *Story* (faith Bp. *Stil-*
" *lingfleet*) they conclude *Timothy* to
" have been only an *Evangelift*, and
" not a fix'd *Bifhop*. But to this,
" faith he, I anfwer That the fre-
" quent *Removes* of *Timothy*, before
" this *Epiftle* to him at *Ephefus*,
" are not material to this purpofe.
" But it is very material to confi-
" der, what *Power* of *Government*

(*i*) *Act.* 18. 18. (*k*) *Act* 18. 19. (*l*) *Act* 19 22
(*m*) *Act.* 20 1. * *Bp.* Stillingfleet's Sermon on 1 *T* 5.
2. *p.* 22, 23.

" St. *Paul* then committed to him,
" which is a certain Proof, that such
" a *Power* was not so peculiar to the
" *Apostles*, by Virtue of their *im-*
" *mediate Commiffion* from *Chrift*,
" but it might be *d legated* to others
" in their ftead. Whether for a lon-
" ger or fhorter time, whether while
" the *Apoftles* went up down, or
" near their Deceafe, makes no dif-
" ference as to the Point of *Delega-*
" *tion*. And if it be granted, that
" fuch an *Apoftolical Power* of *Go-*
" *verning Churches* might be com-
" mitted to others, and was actual-
" ly fo by the *Apoftles*; then there
" is no more to be done, but to en-
" quire, Whether upon their *Remo-*
" *val* or *Departure*, they did en-
" truft any Perfons in fuch a man-
" ner, as it is certain from *Scri-*
" *pture* St. *Paul* did *Timothy*, as to
" the *Churches* of *Afia*, when he
" went into *Macedonia*". Now for
the time in which *Timothy* was made
Bifhop of *Ephefus*, that may be beft
col-

collected from thefe Words, 1 *Tim.*
1. 3. where St. *Paul* relates, that he
befought him to abide ftill at *Ephe-*
fus, when he himfelf went into *Ma-*
cedonia. Now St. *Paul*'s Journey into *Macedonia*, which is here intended, is not that mention'd, *Act.* 16.
for then there was no *Church* of E-
phefus to be *Bifhop* of ; St. *Paul* had
not then feen *Ephefus*, nor planted
any *Church* there till a confiderable
time afterwards (*n*). Neither could
it be when he left *Ephefus*, when he
went the Second time into *Macedo-*
nia, mention'd *Act.* 20. 1. for he had
fent *Timotheus* and *Eraftus* before
him thither, *Act.* 19. 22. But it was
after he had ftay'd three Months in
Greece, when hearing that the *Jews*
laid wait for him, as he went about
to Sail into *Syria*, he chang'd his
Courfe, and purpos'd to return thro'
Macedonia (*o*). Then was the time
when he went into *Macedonia*, that

(*n*) *Act.* 18. 19. & *Act.* 19. 1, 2, 3, &c. (*o*) *Act.* 20. 3.

he

he requir'd or enjoin'd *Timothy* to
go to *Ephesus*, the *Metropolis* of the
Proconsular Asia, and to undertake
the *Government* of that *Church*. To
which when *Timothy* had condescen-
ded, he was sent before with *Sopater*,
Aristarchus and the rest, who all
tarried at *Troas* for the coming of the
Holy Apostle. And 'tis most likely
he was there, when the *Apostle's* first
Epistle came unto his Hands, which
was not written from *Laodicea*, according to the Subscription thereof,
but ἐκ Μακεδονίας, out of *Macedonia*, as
St. *Athanasius* does expresly say *(p)*.
And tho' the *Holy Apostle* did hope
to come unto him shortly *(q)*, and
to instruct him more fully for his
weighty Imployment, yet well consi-
dering how many *Lets* and *Impedi-
ments* might intervene, he thought it
convenient, in the mean time, to
send him that *Instructive Epistle*,
that he might know, how he ought

(p) *Athanas. in Synop. Sacr. Script.* (q) *1 Tim. 3. 14.*

to

to behave himself in the *House* of *God,* which is the *Church* of the living *God,* the *Pillar* and *Ground* of *Truth* (*r*) After this time, I do not find that the *Apostle* did employ *Timothy* in any other *general Service,* which concern'd the *Church* , or that he ever call'd him from *Ephesus,* except that time, when he was to make haft to *Rome,* to be an *Assistant* there to St. *Paul* in that dangerous Exigency. And this was no other, than what St. *Paul* might require, and what *Timothy* might perform, without any manner of *Detraction* from the *Episcopal Dignity* and *Power,* which had been conferred upon him : All the *Epistles,* wherein the Name of *Timothy* is join'd with St. *Paul's,* were written within the compass of two Years, which was fo fhort an abfence from his *Episcopal Charge,* that it might be very eafily difpens'd withal, efpe-

<hr />

(*r*) 1 *Tim.* 3 15.

cial-

cially when the *publick Service* of
the *Church* did so highly require it.
Now several Ancient and Modern
Divines will not have *Timothy* to be
made *Bishop* of the *Church* of E-
phesus, till after St. *Paul*'s coming
to *Rome*, but the Second of the two
E*pistles* doth clearly overthrow that
Opinion, in which the *Holy Apostle*
acquaints *Timothy*, how he had di-
spos'd of his Retinue; *Titus* being
gone into *Dalmatia* (s), *Crescens*
to *Galatia*, E*rastus* taking up his a-
bode at *Corinth*, and *Trophimus* left
at *Miletum* sick ; he also there takes
care to have the *Cloak* and *Parch-
ments*, which were left at *Troas*,
where *Timothy* staid for him, A*ct*.
20. 5. to be sent speedily unto him.
And since that *Timothy* was with St.
Paul at *Troas*, when he went from
thence to *Miletus*, it is a sufficient
Reason, why he did not address himself to him, but to the *Bishops* and

(s) 2 *Tim* 4. 10. *Taking it, as it seemeth, in his way to*
Crete.

Pres-

Presbyters of the *leſſer Aſia*, who came from *Epheſus*, where they were gather'd together, and expected the *Orders* and *Directions* of the *Holy Apoſtle :* " Theſe were the
" Men (ſaith Bp. *Stillingfleet* *)
" whom he then put in mind of
" their *Duty* by his *Speech*, as he
" had done *Timothy* by an E*piſtle*
" not long before directed to him.
" Whoſe *Office* was no more ſuperſe-
" ded by this *Charge* given to them ,
" than a *Proconſuls* was by the *Se-*
" *nate*'s *Inſtructions* to his *Legats*,
" when himſelf was preſent. If it
" were evidently prov'd,that St.*Paul*
" then carry'd away *Timothy* with
" him to *Jeruſalem*, and ſo to *Rome*,
" there would be greater Force in
" the *Objection*. But how doth that
" appear ? Not from *Scripture.* For
" when St. *Paul* appear'd at the *Tem-*
" *ple*, the *Jews* laid hold on him,
" becauſe they ſuppos'd he had

---

* *Bp.* Stillingfleet'*s Sermon on* 1 T*im.* 5.22. *p.* 24, 25.

.

G   " brought

" brought *Trophimus* the *Ephesian*
" with him into the *Temple*, whom
" they had seen so much with him
" in the City, *Act.* 21. 29. How
" came *Timothy* not to be as much
" taken notice of, if he were there?
" For he being discover'd by the
" *Jews* of *Asia*, there was far great-
" er Reason for them to have rais'd
" a Tumult about *Timothy*, than a-
" bout *Trophimus*. After this we
" find St. *Paul* kept Two Years in
" Prison, *Act.* 24. 27. and not a
" word of *Timothy*, whom we
" may justly suppose exercising his
" *Charge* all that time at *Ephesus*.
" When St.*Paul* was carry'd to *Rome*,
" we find not *Timothy* in his Com-
" pany; no mention being made of
" him till he wrote the *Epistles* to
" the *Philippians* *(t)*, and to the
" *Colossians* (*u*), and then *Timothy*
" was with him. For St. *Paul* had
" sent for him from *Ephesus* in his

(*t*) *Phil.* 1. 1. (*u*) *Coloss.* 1. 1.

" Second

" Second E*piſtle* (*w*); where in
" all probability, he remain'd till
" that time. During his ſtay at
" *Rome* thoſe E*piſtles* were written,
" as likewiſe that to *Philemon,*and to
" the *Hebrews* ; in which it is ſaid,
" That he had been Impriſon'd, and
" was then at Liberty (*x*); and in-
" tended ſhortly to return into the
" E*aſtern* Parts. From hencefor-
" wards we read nothing of *Timothy*
" in *Scripture.* But St. *Jerome*
" makes him *Biſhop* of the *Epheſi-*
" *ans* (*y*), and ſo doth Eu*ſebius*
" (*z*); *Theodoret* calls him, *the A-*
" *poſtle of thoſe in Aſia* (*a*); and
" St. *Chryſoſtom* ſaith, *The whole*
" *People of Aſia were committed to*
" *his Charge* (*b*), *i. e.* of this *Pro-*
" *conſular Aſia,* which lay about
" *Epheſus*". So that *Timothy* could
not be then in the *Office* of an E*van-*
geliſt, which was to expire when

(*w*) 2 *Tim.*4.9. (*x*) *Heb.* 13.23. (*y*) *Hier. in Ca-*
tal. (*z*) *Euſeb. Hiſt. Eccleſ. l.* 3. *cap* 4. (*a*) *Theod, in*
1 *Tim.* 3.1 (*b*) *Chryſ in* 1 *Tim* 5.19 *Hom.* 15.

Chri-

Christianity was every where Planted, but he muſt be in the *Sacred Order* and *Office* of *Epiſcopacy*, which was to continue to the end of the World, and this is very plain from theſe Words of the *Holy Apoſtle*, which he ſpake unto *Timothy*, *I charge thee in the ſight of God, and before Jeſus Chriſt, that thou keep this Commandment without ſpot, and unreproveable, until the appearing of our Lord Jeſus Chriſt* (c). Now *Timothy* was not like to live till *Chriſt*'s ſecond coming to *Judgment*, therefore the *Charge* here given by the *Apoſtle*, was not Perſonal only, but ſuch as was to appertain to him, and to his *Succeſſors* for ever, even till the appearing of our Lord and Saviour *Jeſus Chriſt*. Thus having fully prov'd that *Timothy* was *Biſhop* of *Epheſus*, and before-hand having made it apparent that *Titus* was *Biſhop* of *Crete*, I have nothing far-

(c) 1 *Tim.* 6. 14.

ther

ther to add upon this Head, than only to make this Enquiry; Whether the *Apostles* upon their Removal from *particular Churches*, did pass this *Power* over to others, as St. *Paul* did plainly in the Case of *Timothy* and *Titus:* And this is such a *Matter of Fact*, that it can have no stronger Proof, than the general Sense of the *Christian Church* in the *Ages* next succeeding the *Apostles*. And first let us see the *Testimonies* of St. *Irenæus*, who not only relates a *Succession* of Persons to the *Apostles* : but he saith, *The Apostles committed the Care of the Churches to them, and left them to succeed in their Places* (*d*): Which implies, that as the *Apostles* themselves had the Care of the *Church*, so they committed it to the *Bishops*, whom they chose to succeed them, and in those *Chairs*

(*d*) *Habemus annumerare eos qui ab Apostolis instituti sunt Episcopi in Ecclesiis――――quibus etiam ipsas Ecclesias committebant――――quos & Successores relinquebant, suum ipsorum locum Magisterii tradentes.*

G 3　　　　　there

there were feveral *Succeffions*, during the Lives of the *Apoftles.* And ftrange it is, that St. *John* who tells us of fo many *Antichrifts,* 1 *Joh.* 2. 18. fhould not tell us of *Epifcopacy* being *Antichriftian,* if he had had the *Spirit* of our prefent times to have believ'd it fuch; which certainly he did not believe, for St. *Irenæus* affures us, that in his younger Years, he faw St. *Polycarp, Bifhop* of *Smyrna,* whom he knew to be fo conftituted by the *Apoftles* (*e*), among which *Apoftles,* *Tertullian* doth expreflv fay that St. *John* was one (*f*). And the fame St. *Irenæus* doth alfo affirm, that *Linus, Cletus* and *Clemens* were made *Bifhops* of *Rome* fucceflively by St. *Peter* and St. *Paul,* and to this *Clemens,* who had *Epifcopatum adminiftrandæ Ecclefiæ, i.e.* the *Epifcopal Power of Governing*

(*e*) Καὶ Πολύκαρπος ὃ ἐν μόνον ὑπὸ Ἀποστόλων μαθητευθεὶς, ἠ συναναστραφεὶς πολλοῖς τοῖς τὸν Χειστὸν ἑωρακόσιν, ἀλλὰ ἠ ὑπὸ Ἀποστόλων κατασταθεὶς εἰς τὴν Ἀσίαν ἐν τῇ ἐν Σμύρνῃ ἐκκλησίᾳ Ἐπίσκοπος ὃ ἠ ἡμεῖς ἑωράκαμεν ἐν τῇ πρώτῃ ἡμῶν ἡλικίᾳ Iren. lib. 3. cap 3. (*f*) *Tertul. de Præfcript. c* 32.

the

the *Church*, there did fucceed *Eva-*
riftus, who liv'd almoft an hundred
Years after *Chrift*, and divided *Rom*
into Seven Parifhes, whofe *Pr... y-*
ters were all under his *Jurifdiction*.
And then to this *Evariftus* fucceeded
Alexander, and *Sixtus*, and feveral
others down to *Eleutherius*, who
was the Twelfth *Bifhop* of *Rome*, after St. *Peter* and St. *Paul* had founded that *Church* (*g*). " So that
" what *Authority* St. *Polycarp* had at
" *Smyrna*, or *Clemens* at *Rome*, th
" faid *Tertullian* faith, the *Bifhops*
" had in other *Churches* (*h*). And
" St. *Chryfoftom* faith of St. *Ignati-*
" *us*, That he receiv'd the *Govern-*
" *ment* of the *Church* of *Antioch*,
" from the *Holy Apoftles* own
" Hands (*i*). And the *Commenta-*

(*g*) *...obus Apoftolis Petro & Paulo Romæ fundata &*
conft utæ Ecclefiæ,——Lino Epifcopatum adminiftrandæ Ec-
*cl... x tradiderunt.——Succedit autem ei Anacletus, 1 *
Cletus poft cum tertio loco ab Apoftolis Epifcopatum fortit..
Clemens,——Huic autem Clementi fuccedit Evariftus, &
Evarifto Alexander, &c——Nunc duodecimo loco Epifco-
patum ab Apoftolis habet Eleutherius. Iren. lib. 3. cap. 3.
(*h*) *Tertull. de Præfcript. c.* 32. (*i*) *Chryfoftom. Tom* 5.
p. 499.

G 4 " tor

" tor on the *Apocalypfe*, under St.
" *Ambrofe*'s Name, calls the *Angels*
" of the *Seven Churches* the Gover-
" *nours* of thofe *Churches*. From
" all which, we may juftly infer,
" That this *Succeffion* was not in
" *meer Prefidency* of *Order*, but
" that the *Bifhops* fucceeded the *A-*
" *poftles* in the *Government* over
" thofe *Churches*. And as *Theodo-*
" *ret* well obferves, The Name of
" *Apoftles* was not continu'd out of
" Reverence to the *Apoftles*; but the
" Name of *Bifhops* was then appro-
" priated to the *Succeffors* of the *Apo-*
ftles.Now that the *Bifhops* did fucceed
" the *Apoftles* (faith Bp.*Stillingfleet**)
" is according to the general Con-
" fent of the *Ancient Fathers* (*k*),
" who were the moft *competent Wit-*
" *neffes* in this Cafe; and is an Ar-
" gument, that they believ'd the *A-*

---

* Bp. *Stillingfleet's Sermon on* 1 *Tim* 5 22   (*k*) *Iren. l.*
3. *c.* 3. *Tertull. de Præfcript. c.* 32. *&* 36. *Cyprian. Epift.*
3. 66. *ed. Oxon. Hier. in Pfal.* 44. *ad Evagr. Epift.* 85 *ad*
Marcell. Aug. in Pfal. 44. *Ambrof. in Eph.* 4. 11. *& in*
1 *Cor.* 12. 28.

" the

" *poftolical Power,* with refpect 'to
" the *Government* of *Churches,* did
" not expire with the *Apoftles,* but
" was to continue as long as *Chrift*
" had promis'd to be with them,
" *i. e.* to the end of the World.
" *Matth.* 28. 20.

Pfeud. * *You fay,* Philalethes, *that*
Diocefan Bifhops *did fucceed the* A-
poftles : *Did the* Presbyters *alfo fucceed the* Seventy Difciples ?

Phil. The *Primitive Church* did
ever believe, that *Diocefan Bifhops*
were the ordinary *Succeffors* of the
Holy Apoftles, and that the *Presbyters* did come in Place of the *Seventy Difciples.* For how can any Rational Man ever imagine, that our
Bleffed Lord, the chief *Shepherd* and
Bifhop of our *Souls,* having made
fuch a *Settlement,* while he was upon Earth, fhould leave his *Church*
uniettl'd and unprovided after he
was gone, with whom he promis'd
to be even to the end of the World;

---

* Mr. *J. W's Letters, p.* 29.

or that he should not perpetuate thofe *Functions* and *Orders*, which himfelf had appointed? So that what the *Holy Apoftles* were in the *Chri-ftian Church*, that are *Diocefan Bi-fhops* ever fince; and what Rank the *Seventy Difciples* held in the *Church* then, the fame and no other do our *Presbyters* hold now.

Pfeud. [*] *You fay that the* Diocefan (*to whom you are pleas'd to appro-priate the Name of* Bifhop) *is the* Apoftles Succeffor, *&c. and there-fore that* Ordination *is his Peculiar: I demand, are thefe the* Succeffors *of the Apoftles* quâ tales *in the very* Apoftolick Office *or not?*

Phil. Diocefan Bifhops did not fuc-ceed the *Holy Apoftles* in their *Ex-traordinary* and *Temporary Prero-gatives*, but in their *Ordinary* and *Permanent Miniftrations*; not in their *Extraordinary* and *Temporary Prerogatives*, as an *Immediate Mif-*

---

[*] Mr. *J. W*'s *Letters*, p. 29.

fion

fion from *Jefus Chrift*, an *Infallible Affurance* of his *Truth*, a *Vifible Affiftance* of his *Spirit*, a *mighty Power* of *working Miracles*, and of *fpeaking with divers Tongues*, all which Peculiars did expire with their Perfons, being only neceffary to the *Planting*, not to the *Perpetuating* of the *Chriftian Church*. But, in the *Ordinary* and *Permanent Miniftrations* of the *Holy Apoftlefhip*, as *Preaching the Word, Difcipling by Baptifm, Confecrating the Eucharift, Excommunicating the Scandalous, Abfolving the Penitent, Governing by Difcipline*, and *Ordaining to the Priefthood*, *Diocefan Bifhops* did fucceed the *Apoftles*; and the great *Neceffities* of the *Church* do require that fuch a *Succeffion* fhould continue even to the Second Coming of our *Bleffed Saviour.*

Pfeud. *I wonder*, **Philalethes**, *that fuch a zealous Affertor* of Diocefan Epifcopacy, *as you, fhould fo ftrangely differ in your Opinion from the*
Learn-

Learned Dr. Hammond : †*He faith,
the there is no* Evidence *for any*
Subject-Presbyters *in* Scripture *times
(as you may fee, if you pleafe to
confult him). And if fo, how did
the* Apoftles *or* Apoftolick Men *pre-
fide over the* primitive Presbyters *?
*Did they take themfelves to be rela-
ted to this or that particular* Diocefe,
as the Paftor *thereof in Peculiar,
efteeming it their* Church. *or* Chair,
fo as one Apoftle *had one* Diocefe *al-
lotted for his Care ; another* Apoftle *another* Diocefe *for his ? Did
they keep within the Limits of any*
Diftrict, *in the Exercife of their* A-
poftolick Function, *fo as to have lefs*
Power *in another ? If you can produce any appearance of* Proof *for
this,* I *fhall (I hope) be able to
confute it, as foon as it is produc'd.
If you mean not fuch a* Prefidency *as*

† *Mr.* J. W*'s Letters,* p. 33. * *Obferve the craft of* Pfeudocheus, *he believes with* Dr Hammond, *that there were no*
Subject-Presbyters *in Scripture Times, but he does not tell us
with* Dr. Hammond, *that thefe were* Bifhops *of the feveral*
Cities *that were in* Judea, *and not* Presbyters *of* Jerufalem.

this,

this, you had as good say nothing :
For 'tis such which de Facto *is now*
in use, but by what Right, *is not easi-*
ly said.

Phil. Indeed, Sir, I have a profound esteem and value for the Name
and Memory of the Excellent and
Learned Dr. *Hammond,* but yet by
no means can I agree with him in his
Annotations upon *Act.* 11. *verf.* 30.
where he faith, " That the Word
" Πρεσβύτεροι, *Elders* or *Priests,* did
" in *Scripture-times* belong princi-
" pally, if not alone, to *Bifhops,*
" there being no Evidence, that any
" of that *Second Order* were then In-
" ftituted ; And he there alfo tells us,
" that St. *James* the Brother of our
" *Lord,* being foon after *Christ's Af-*
" *cenfion* conftituted *Bifhop* of the
" *Church* of *Jerufalem,* the *Deacons*
" are the firft that are added to him,
" *Acts* 6. and no mention as yet of
" any *middle Order*". So that according to Dr. *Hammond's* Senti-
ments, the Πρεσβύτεροι, the *Elders* or
Priests

Priests here mention'd, were not the
Elders or *Priests* of *Jerusalem*, that
one City, but the *Bishops* of the several Cities that were in *Judea*. Now,
Sir, if you espouse his *Opinion*, as
you would seem to do, how can you
affert that St. *Paul* and St. *Barnabas*
were *Ordain'd* by *Presbyters*, when
you say with him, that there were
none of that *Second Order* in *Scripture-times*? You ought to have settled your *Hypothesis* upon firmer
Principles, and not after this manner to contradict and overthrow it:
All that you can plead in your Vindication, is this, that you have had
the Misfortune to be miftaken with
fuch a celebrated and learned *Author*.
'Tis evident from *Acts* 21. 19. that
there were *fixed Presbyters* in the
Church of *Jerusalem*, for 'tis there
faid, that St. *Paul* went unto *James*,
and all the *Elders* were prefent.
They muft therefore refide in that
City, for there was not Sufficient
time to Summon them from all Parts
of

of the Country. And therefore the
Enemies of *Epifcopal Superiority* are
fo far from gaining any Advantage
to their Caufe by proving thefe *Pref-
byters* Affembled at *Jerufalem* to be
no *Bifhops*, that it is a plain Demon-
ftration of the true *Primitive Government* of the *Church* from clear and
exprefs *Apoftolical Practice*, viz. **A**
Bifhop, with his *Subject-Presbyters*,
refiding in the *City* or *Church* of *Jerufalem*. For how can you imagine,
that fuch a Number of *Chriftian Converts*, as there were in *Jerufalem*, could
ever be crouded into one *Congregation*, but that the greateft part of them
muft be under the Care and Inftructions of the *Jerufalem-Presbyters*, who
were all of them under St. *James* the
Bifhop of that *Church?* And that you
may not in the leaft queftion the
Truth of what I now fay, I'll plainly prove,

1. That the *Apoftle* St. *James the
Lefs*, who is alfo called the *Juft*, and
the Brother of our *Lord*, was the firft
Diocefan

Diocefan Bifhop of the *Church* of *Je-rufalem* (*l*).

And then 2*dly.* That there were many *Presbyters* in the *Church* of *Jerufalem,* the *Paſtors* and *Teachers* of feveral *Congregations* in that City, and all of them were under St. *James's Epifcopal* Care and Government.

1. That St. *James* the Apoſtle was *Diocefan Bifhop* of *Jerufalem,* appears very plainly from the *Holy Scriptures.* When St. *Peter* was deliver'd from his Imprifonment by the Angel, he faid to thofe that were furpriz'd and aſtonifh'd at his Prefence, Go *and fhew thefe things to* James *and to the Brethren,* Act. 12. 17. In which Words the Deference

_____

(*l*) *St.* James *was Sirnam'd the* Juſt *for his many eminent Vertues, and to diſtinguiſh him from the other* Apoſtle *of the fame Name, he was call'd* James the Lefs, *the Son of* Alpheus, *who was the fame with* Cleophas; *for* Mary *the Mother of* James the Lefs *is by St.* John *call'd* Mary *the Wife of* Cleophas. *Compare thefe Texts,* Matth. 10. 3. Mar. 15. 40. Mar. 16. 1. Joh. 19. 25. Gal. 1. 19. *So that St.* James, *being our* Lord's Coufin-German, *is call'd his* Brother, *according to an ordinary Expreffion in the* Sacred Dialect.

paid

paid to St. *James* is vifible, and taken notice of elfewhere frequently,
as *Gal.* 1. 19. *Gal.* 2. 1, 9. but moft
of all, *Act.* 15. 13, 19. Where you
may obferve, that fome *Chriftians* of
Judea about the Year 51, coming
down to *Antioch* in *Syria*, fhewed
their Zeal extremely for the *Jewifh*
Rites and *Ceremonies*, which were
as yet Tolerated in the *Chriftian*
Church; and as if they had been neceffary to Salvation, impos'd them
upon the *Gentile Converts*, without
any Order or Advice from St. *James*,
or any other of the *Apoftles*. Thefe
Doctrines St. *Paul* and St. *Barnabas*
endeavour'd to refute by *Difputati-*
on, but when all they could do pro-
ved unfuccefsful, the *Church* of *An-*
tioch agreed to fend St. *Paul* and St.
Barnabas to *Jerufalem*, to the *Apo-*
ftles and *Presbyters*, who did meet
in *Council*, and confult about this
Matter.

In the Determination of this Bufinefs, tho' St. *Peter* and others pro-
H pounded

pounded their *Judgment*, yet St. *James's Authority* (m), who was *Bishop* of *Jerusalem*, did sway all so far*, that they all submitted to it; and according to his Direction, a *Letter* was sent to the People of *Antioch*, to pacifie their Minds, and settle their Practice for the future. Now this was eleven Years after St. *Paul's* first sight of St. *James*, and fourteen Years after his *Conversion*; and then nine Years after this, being the 58th of *Christ's Nativity*, St. *Paul* makes his last Journey to *Jerusalem*, where still he finds St. *James*. *And the day following* Paul *went in with us unto* James ; *and all the Elders* (that is *Presbyters*) *were present, Act.* 21. 18. So that for twenty Years together, we have apparent Evidence in *Scripture* of St. *James's* Residing at

---

(*m*) *Act.* 15. 13. James *answered, saying, Men and Brethren, hearken unto me.*——*v.*19.*Wherefore my Sentence is,*—— or *I determine.* * 'Εγὼ κείνω. *Illud* ἐγὼ *cum Emphasi proferendum.* Vid. Jo. Pricæi Annot. in Loc. *Sic* κεί ἐιν ἐείσι, litem discernere, *to determine a Controversie.* apud Demosth.

Jerusalem, as *Bishop* of that *Church.*
And indeed there is scarce any *Ancient Writer,* but what gives a full *Attestation* to this *Truth.* For *Eusebius* out of St. *Clemens* doth tell us,
That St. *James* was made *Bishop* of *Jerusalem* by the *Apostles,* μετὰ τὴν ἀνάληψιν τῦ σωτῆρος, after the *Ascension* of our *Saviour* (*n*). Then also St. *Jerome* as plainly from *Hegesippus,* *statim post Passionem Domini,* immediately after the *Passion* of our *Lord* (*o*). And *Epiphanius,* for his greater *Credit,* makes him not only the first *Bishop* that ever was, *adv. Hæres.* 29. *n.* 3. but *Bishop* of the *Lord's own Throne,* ᾧ πεπίστευκε κύριος τὸν θρόνον αὐτῦ ἐπὶ τῆς γῆς, and that too by the *Lord's* Appointment (*p*). Add to these the joint Consent and Suffrage of 289 Bishops in the *Sixth General Council* of *Constantinople,* who did all affirm, That St. *James,* the *Lord's* Brother, was the first *Bishop* of *Jeru-*

(*n*) *Ecclef. Hist. l.* 2. *c.* 1. (*o*) *In Script. Ecclef.* (*p*) *Epiphan. adv Hæres.* 78. *n.* 7.

falem (*q*). Now these are sufficient *Testimonies*, and we need not to
bring any more from *Holy Scripture*,
Fathers or *Councils*, since our Adverfaries themselves do freely confefs,
that the fame St. *James* was the firft
Bifhop of *Jerufalem*, the *Metropolis*
of the *Jews*. Thus *Blondel* declares,
That all the *Ancients* do conftantly
affert, that *James* the Brother of our
Lord was *Ordain'd* by his *Colleagues*
Bifhop of the *Church* of *Jerufalem*
(*r*). And *Salmafius* tells us, That
St. *James* ftirr'd not from *Jerufa-*
lem, tho' the other *Apoftles* were
fcatter'd and difpers'd to Plant the
Holy Gofpel in other Countries (*s*).
Nay *Calvin* himfelf grants all that
we plead for, in his *Commentaries*
on *Gal.* 2. 9. He faith, That St. *James*
was preferr'd to St. *Peter*, becaufe
he was *Ecclefiæ Hierofolymitanæ Præ-*

(*q*) *Concil. Conftantinop. in Can.* 32. (*r*) *Blondel in A-*
polog. p 50. *Jacobum Domini Fratrem Hierofolymitanæ Ec-*
clefiæ Epifcopum à Collegis ordinatum conftanter afferunt ve-
teres omnes. (*s*) *Hierofolymis non abftitit, nec quoquam ex-*
tra Urbem pedem movit. Wal. Meffal. p. 20.

fectus,

fectus, Governour of the Church of *Jerusalem*. Now for the Time that St. *James* continu'd *Bishop* of *Jerusalem*, we do find that St. *Jerome* does declare, That this Blessed Apostle and *Bishop* was Martyr'd in the seventh Year of *Nero* (*Anno Christi* 63.) *postquam triginta annos Hierosolymis rexerat Ecclesiam*; after he had been *Bishop* of *Jerusalem* thirty Years (*t*). And when St. *James* was dead, then *Simeon* the Son of *Cleophas*, one of our *Saviour's Disciples* and Kindred, was made the *Bishop* of that *Church*, St. *Peter*, St. *Paul*, and St. *John*, and others of the Apostles being then alive, and all consenting to it (*u*). He liv'd to a great Age, and *Epiphanius* in his Catalogue of the *Bishops* of *Jerusalem*, reckons first St. *James*, and next *Simeon*, who was Crucify'd under *Trajan* (*w*).

(*t*) *Hieron. de Script. Ecclef.* (*u*) *Eufeb. Ecclef. Hift*, *l. 3. c. 10.* (*w*) *Epiphan. Hæref. 66.*

H 3 Thus

Thus you fee, *Pfeudocheus*, That St. *James the Lefs*, one of the twelve *Apoftles*, was *Diocefan Bifhop* of the *Church* of *Jerufalem*; and kept conftantly within his *Diftrict*, in the Exercife of his *Epifcopal Function*. And this being fo very clear; I know not what better *Form* of *Government* we can have, than that which was Eftablifh'd at *Jerufalem* in the firft *Chriftian Church* that ever was, and of which fome of the Kindred of our *Saviour* had the *Adminiftration*.

And now 2*dly*. I come to fhew, That there were many *Presbyters* in the *Church* of *Jerufalem*, the *Paftors* and *Teachers* of feveral *Congregations* in that City, and all of them under St. *James*'s *Epifcopal Care* and *Government*. After our Bleffed *Saviour* had chofen the *twelve Apoftles*, he appointed other *Seventy* alfo, and fent them Two and Two before him to prepare his Way. Of thefe the *Lord* made choice of fome to be *Prophets*, and others to be *Evange-lifts*,

lifts, fome to be *Pastors* and *Teach-ers,* and others to be *Helps* in Go-vernment, according to the Meafure and the Purpofe of his *Grace* be-ftow'd upon them, in the Effufion of his *Spirit,* 1 *Cor.* 12. & *Eph.* 4. 8. Now out of thefe thus qualify'd and prepar'd for the *Work* of *God,* there were feveral appointed to affift St. *James,* in the difcharge of that great *Truft* committed to him, by the u-nanimous Confent of the *Holy Apo-ftles.* And St. *Ignatius* does tell us, That there were *Presbyters* in the *Church* of *Jerufalem,* before the E-lection of the *Seven Deacons,* for faith he, St. *Stephen* did minifter; Ἰακώβῳ καὶ τοῖς Πρεσβυτέροις, &c. to *James* and to the *Presbyters* (*x*). Now thefe *Presbyters* are mention'd by the Name of *Elders,* in three feve-ral Chapters of the *Acts of the Apo-ftles,* during the time that St. *James* was *Bifhop* of that *Church.* The firft

(*x*) *Ignat. ep. ad Heron.*

H 4

men-

mention of them is in *Act.* 11. 30.
where we read, That when the *Difciples*, which dwelt at *Antioch*, had
made a Contribution for the Brethren of *Judea*, they fent it to the
Elders (*i. e.* the *Presbyters*) of *Jerufalem* by the Hands of *Barnabas*
and *Saul*. The fecond Mention of
thefe *Presbyters* is in *Act.* 15. 4. and
in the 6, 22, 23 Verfes of that Chapter. Then the third Mention of
thefe *Jerufalem-Presbyters* is in *Act.*
21. 18. and there St. *Luke* relates,
That St. *Paul* at his laft going to *Jerufalem*, went in unto *James*, and
that all the *Elders* (*i, e.* the *Pref-
byters*) were prefent; and he alfo
tells you, what Counfel and Advice
they gave him, how he might ingra-
tiate himfelf with the *Jews*. Here
we find St. *James* the Bifhop attend-
ed by his *Presbyters*, at the Reception
of St. *Paul* : and they together joining
with him in the Confultation then in
hand, the *Bufinefs* being *great* and
weighty. And indeed there was a
great

great Neceſſity, that ſeveral *Presbyters* ſhould be reſident at *Jeruſalem,*
ſince there were among ſuch large
Numbers of *Chriſtian Converts* (as
we have all the Reaſon imaginable to
believe) a great many ſeveral *Congregations*; for we read in *Act.* 2.
41. That there were Three Thouſand
Perſons converted at St. *Peter*'s firſt
Sermon. And again in *Act.* 4. 4. we
find that many of them which heard
the Word, (then *Preach'd,* not in a
Set Aſſembly, but occaſionally in the
Temple) believ'd ; and the Number
of the Men was about Five Thouſand.
And then in *Act.* 5. 14. St. *Luke*
ſaith, That *Believers* were the more
added to the *Church*, Multitudes
both of Men and Women. Then
ſtill there were greater Additions
made to the *Church,* as we find in
Act. 6. 7. That the Number of the
Diſciples multiply'd in *Jeruſalem*
greatly; and a great Company of
the *Prieſts,* or as the *Syriac* reads it,
of the *Jews,* were obedient, or ſub-
mit-

mitted to the *Faith*. But there remains yet another Inftance, that's more decifive; For St. *James* and the *Elders* (*i. e.* the *Presbyters*) of *Jerufalem* obferve to St. *Paul*, That there were many *Myriads* of the *Circumcifion* which believed. *Thou feeft Brother how many Thoufands [Myriads] of* Jews *there are which believe, and they are all zealous of the Law* (*y*). And now after all thefe Acceffions, what manner of *Church* fhall we conceive this to be, a *Congregational* one, fhall all thefe Thoufands make but one *Affembly* for *Communion* in *Prayer*, and the *Sacraments ?* 'Tis Incredible. There was no Place in *Jerufalem* that was large enough to hold them, there were, as I faid before, many feveral *Congregations*, and this *Church* was no other than a *Diocefe*, which was *Govern'd* by St. *James*, and *Taught* by his *Presbyters*.

(*y*) *Act*. 21. 20. Θεωρεῖς ἀδελφε, πόσαι Μυειάδις εἰσὶν Ιαδαίων τ πεπιςευκότων. *Confpicis frater, quot decem millia Judæorum credentium.* Ar. Mont.
                                                            Pfeud.

Pſeud. *I could never have thought,* Philalethes, *that ſuch an exaƐt Plat-form of* Dioceſan Epiſcopacy *could ever have been produc'd from the* Holy Scriptures; *theſe indeed ſeem to be very rational Obſervations, and I could wiſh that you would oblige me with ſome more Teſtimonies of this .Nature from* Sacred Writ.

Phil. Such Favours, Sir, ſhall be as readily granted, as requeſted ; and if you pleaſe to conſider, you'll find that there were ſeveral *Churches* in the *Apoſtles times,* which had many *Presbyters* that labour'd in the Word, over whom *ApoſŧIes* or *Apoſtolick Men* did preſide. This the *Holy Scriptures* do plainly at-teſt ; In the *Church* of *Epheſus, AƐt.* 20. 17. in the *Church* of *Rome, Rom.* 16. of *Corinth,* 1 *Cor.* 14. 29. of *Phi-lippi, Phil.* 1. 1. of *Theſſalonica,* 1 *Theſſ.* 5. 12. of other *Churches* the like is affirm'd, *Heb.* 13. 17. St. *James* 5: 14. 1 St. *Pet.* 5. 1. Now by *God*'s perpetual Ordinance, as your ſelves
con⸱

confeſs, there muſt be one chief *Pa-ſtor* of each *Presbytery*, to guide as well the *Presbyters* that are *Teachers*, as the *Flock*, that are *Hearers:* Tell me then, what Difference betwixt chief *Paſtors* eſtabliſh'd in every Ci-ty, by *God's Law*, as you are forc'd to grant; and the *Biſhops* ſucceed-ing the *Apoſtles* in their *Churches* and *Chairs*, as the *Fathers* affirm (*z*). If you diſlike the Word *Biſhop* it is *Catholick* and *Apoſtolick* ; if you diſlike the *Office*, it is *God's Ordi-nance*, by the Aſſertion of your own *Party.* For *Beza* does make it an *Eſſential* and *Perpetual* Part of *God's Ordinance* to have one *Chief* in eve-ry *Presbytery.*

His Words are theſe, *Eſſentiale fu-it in eo de quo hic agimus, quod ex Dei Ordinatione perpetua neceſſe fu-it, eſt, & erit, ut in Presbyterio*

(*z*) *Euſeb. Chron. Hieron. Interprete. Theodoret. in Phi-lip. 2. 15.* Ἐπαφρόδιτον ὑμῶν Ἀπόσολον——Τὲς νῦν κφλυμένες, Ἐπισκόπες Ἀπόσολες ὠνόμαζον. *Thoſe very Perſons were call'd* Apoſtles, *whom by Uſage of* Speech, *the Church now caſs* Biſhops.

quiſ-

quiſpiam & loco & dignitate primus,
actioni gubernandæ præſit, cum eo,
quod ipſi attributum eſt jure (a).
This was Eſſential in the Matter we
have in Hand, that by *God's Ordi-*
nance which muſt always endure, it
has been, is and ſhall be needful,
that in the *Presbytery* one *Chief* in
Place and *Dignity,* ſhould moderate
and rule every Action, with that
Right which is allow'd him by *God's*
Law. Yea, *Calvin* himſelf ſays, *Nec*
humanum eſt Inventum, ſed Dei ipſi-
us Inſtitutum, quod ſingulis ſuas aſ-
ſignamus Eccleſias. Paulus Archip-
pum Coloſſenſium Epiſcopum comme-
morat (b). It is not Man's Device,
but the very *Ordinance* of *God,* that
we aſſign to every Man his *Church.*
Paul himſelf mentions *Archippus,*
Biſhop of *Coloſſus.* And *Calvin* further ſays, That *Equality* breeds *Fa-*
ctions (c). " *Subordination* then

(a) *In Reſponſ. ad Tractat. de Miniſtror. Evangel. Gra-*
tibus. Cap 22. Fol 153. (b) *Calv Inſtitut. lib. 4. cap. 3.*
c) *Calv. Inſtitut. lib 4 cap. 4.*

" in

" in some, and *Superiority* in o-
" thers *, is as requisite to *Ecclesia-*
" *stical* as *Civil Polity*, without
" which *Schism* becomes as fatal to
" the *Church*, as *Rebellion* is to the
" *State.* So that all of us must sub-
" scribe to the grave *Sentence* and
" *Judgment* of St. *Jerom*; unless
" the *Episcopal Pre-eminence* of *Au-*
" *thority* and *Office* be preserv'd.
" For, saith he, To suppress the
" *Seeds* of *Dissention*, one was set
" above the rest ; otherwise there
" would be, *Tot in Ecclesiis efficien-*
" *ter Schismata*, *quot Sacerdotes*
" (*d*). As many *Schisms* in the
" *Church*, as there are *Presbyters*,
" especially, if every *Presbyter* has
" *Power* of *Ordination* intrinsecal to
" his *Office*, by the *Divine Right* of
" *Apostolical Institution.* For what
" then would be the Use of *Ordinati-*
" *on*, but chiefly to propagate *Schism*

---

* Bp. *Mossom on Matth.* 28. 19, *&c.* (d) *Hieron. a*
Evagr. & contra Luciferanos.

Pseud

Pſeud. * *You ſay, Sir, that there muſt be one chief* Paſtor *in every* Preſbytery, *to guide as well the* Presbyters *that are* Teachers, *as the* Flock *that are* Hearers. *This is very true, and in all* Presbyteries *or* Synods *(whether great or ſmall) 'tis fit, for* Order's *ſake, that there ſhould be a* Preſident *or* Moderator *over the reſt, and it has been our uſual Practice. Now if you will call the* Moderator *of a* Presbytery *by the Name of a* Biſhop, *I ſhall not gain-ſay it, provided you grant the* Presbyters *to be his* Colleagues, *and of the ſame* Office *with him. Such a* Biſhop *as this* Beza *pleads for in the Words by you alledg'd. And as to your Quotation out of* Calvin, *it ſerves not your purpoſe at all; for his aſſerting the* Divine Right *of a* Biſhop *or* Presbyter *over every particular* Church, *is ſo far from favouring* Dioceſan Prelacy *that it is directly contrary to it. But*

* Mr. *J. W's Letters, p.* 34, 37.

if

if you would be contented with such a
Prefidency *or* Epifcopacy, *as the Re-*
verend and truly Learned Bifhop
Ufher *propos'd to King* Charles I. *as*
an expedient to unite the Englifh Pro-
teftants, *and Reform the* Church,
I *believe few of the* Nonconformifts
would refufe to fubmit to it (e).
For my Part, I could readily comply
therewith. But this Excellent Bifhop
in his Book (as is evident from ma-
ny Expreffions *therein*) *fuppofes* Bifhop *and* Presbyter *to be really of the*
fame Office, *and to differ only* Gradu
in Degree; *not* Ordine *in* Order; *as*
if they were of a Diftinct Office.

Phil. Indeed, *Pfeudocheus,* if you
will have your *Moderator* to be a
Bifhop, I fhall not gain-fay it, provided that he be fuch a *Moderator,*
who fhall be a *ftanding Officer,* during Life, to whom all the *Presby-*
ters are to be obedient as to *Chrift,*
that is, to the *Moderator,* as repre-

(e) *Bp.* Ufher's *Reduction of Epifcopacy, in Prefat.* § 1,
2. *and Prop* 1.

fenting

senting the *Person* of *Christ:* That
he be truly *Consecrated,* and under-
stood as the *Principle* of *Unity* in his
Church; so that they, who unjustly
break off from his *Communion ,*
are thereby in a *Schism* ; That he
shew his *Succession* by *Regular Ordination,* convey'd down from the *Holy Apostles.* In short, that he have
all that *Character* and *Authority,*
which we see to have been Recogniz'd
in the *Bishops,* in the very Age of
the *Apostles,* and all the succeeding
Ages of *Christianity* ; and then call
him *Moderator, Superintendent,* or
Bishop : For the Contest is not about
the *Name,* but the *Thing.*

And here I cannot but wonder at
your strange *Misrepresentations* of
Calvin and *Beza,* who, with others
of our *Reformers,* did ever account
it a most unjust *Reproach* upon them,
to think that they condemn'd *Episcopacy*; which they say they did
not throw off, but could not have it
in *Geneva,* without coming under

I   the

the *Papal Hierarchy:* They highly Applauded and Congratulated the *Episcopal Hierarchy* of the *Church of England,* as it appears in their several Letters to Queen *Elizabeth,* to the Archbishop of *Canterbury,* and others of our *English Bishops:* They pray'd heartily to *God* for the *Continuance* and *Preservation* of it: They lamented their own *unhappy Circumstances,* and wish'd for *Episcopacy* in their own *Churches,* the want of which they own'd as a great *Defect*; but call'd it their *Misfortune* rather than their *Fault.* As the Learned of the *French Hugonots* have likewise pleaded in their Behalf. As for their Excuse, I shall not meddle with that, because I think it was not sufficient; They might have had *Bishops consecrated* in other Places, for Archbishop *Cranmer* was fix'd in his See of *Canterbury* three Years before * *John*

* John Calvin *came first to* Geneva *in* 1536. *after some time he was order'd to depart that City, but was recall'd* Sept. 1541. *where he continu'd to his Death, which was in the Year of our Lord,* 1564.

Calvin

Calvin came firſt to *Geneva,* and the *Civil Magiſtrate* would as well have receiv'd *Reform'd Biſhops,* as it did *Presbyters* afterwards. But whatever becomes of their *Excuſe,* 'tis very plain, that they gave their *Suffrage* for E*piſcopacy ,* which whoſo pleaſes may ſee at large in Dr. *Durel's View of the Government and Worſhip in the Reform'd Churches beyond the Seas,* (who was himſelf one of them) Printed, 1662. So that our *Modern Presbyterians* have departed from *Calvin* as well as from *Luther,* in their *Abhorrence* of E*piſcopacy,* from all the *Chriſtian World,* in all Ages ; and particularly from our late *Reformers,* both of one ſort, and of the other. For *John Calvin,* tho' he was never *Ordain'd,* (as *Beza* and *Papirius Maſſonius,* two Writers of his Life, do teſtifie *) yet does he thus deliver himſelf in his *Vindication of the Hierarchy. Talem*

---

* *In Vita Calvini.*

ſi

fi nobis Hierarchiam exhibeant, in qua fic emineant Epifcopi, ut Chrifto fubeffe non recufent, & ab illo tan-quam unico Capite pendeant, & ad ipfum referantur, &c. Tum vero *nullo non Anathemate dignos fatear, fi qui erunt, qui non Eam reverenter, fummaq; Obedientiâ obfervent (f).* If they would give us fuch an *Hierarchy*, in which the *Bifhops* fhould fo excel, as that they did not refufe to be fubject to *Chrifl*, and to depend upon him, as their only Head, and refer all to Him; then I will confefs, that they are worthy of all *Anathema's*, if any fuch fhall be found, who will not Reverence it, and fubmit themfelves to it, with the utmoft Obedience*. And *Beza* fuppofes as pofitively as *Calvin*, That there were none that would oppofe the *Epifco-pal Hierarchy*; and he condemns them as Mad-men, if any fuch could

(f) *Calvin. de Neceffitat. Ecclef. Reformand*   * Calvin *little thought what a perverfe Spirit would hereafter arife in our* Englifh Fanaticks.

be

be found.   For thus faith he in that very Book which he wrote against *Seravia,* a Prebend of *Canterbury. Si qui funt autem (quod fane mihi non facile perfuaferis) qui omnem Epifcoporum Ordinem rejiciant, abfit ut quifquam fatis fanæ Mentis furoribus illorum affentiatur* (g).   If there be any fuch (which you fhall hardly perfwade me to believe) who reject the whole O1 *der* of Epifcopacy; *God* forbid that any Man in his Wits, fhould affent to the Madnefs of fuch Men.   And then afterwards he goes on and faith, *Quod fi nunc Ecclefiæ inftauratæ Anglicanæ fuorum Epifcoporum & Archiepifcoporum Authoritate fuffultæ perftant, quemadmodum hoc illis noftrâ memoriâ contigit, ut ejus Ordinis Homines non tantum Infignes Dei Martyres, fed etiam præftantiffimos Doctores & Paftores habuerit,* &c. (h).   If the *Reformed Churches* of *England* remain

(g) *Beza de Grad. Minift. Evang. c.* 1.   (h) *Ibidem c.* 18.

ftill

ftill fupported with the Authority
of their *Archbifhops* and *Bifhops*, as
it hath come to pafs in our Memory, that they have had Men of that
Rank, not only famous *Martyrs*,
but moſt excellent *Doctors* and *Paſtors*, *&c.* And then he calls the *Hierarchy* a Singular Bleſſing of *God*,
*& Fruatur ſane iſta ſingulari Dei be-
neficentia, quæ utinam ſit illi Perpetua* (*i*)*:* and wiſhes that the *Church*
may ever enjoy it. So that you,
Pſeudocheus, and the *Modern Prcf-
byterians*, are difarm'd of the *Pre-
cedent* of *Calvin* and *Beza*, and all
the *Reformers* abroad, by whoſe
Sentence ye are *Anathematiz'd*, and
counted as Mad-men. And now that
you fpeak of Archbiſhop *Uſher*'s *Reduction of* Epiſcopacy *to the Form of
Synodical Government*, pray take this
Account of it from his Grace's then
Chaplain, Dr. *Nicholas Bernard*,
fometime Preacher to the Honoura-

(*i*) *Beza de Grad. Miniſt. Evang. c.* 18.

ble

ble Society of *Grays-Inn, London.*
In that Book of his Entitled, *Clavi
Trabales, pag.* 54. he there faith,
" As for that of his *Reduction* of
" Epifcopacy to the *Form* of *Syno-*
" *dical Government, &c.* prefented
" to his late Majefty of *Bleffed Me-*
" *mory, Anno* 1641. It is to be con-
" fider'd, how it was occafion'd by
" the prefent *Tempeftuous Violence*
" of the *Times,* as an Accommoda-
" tion by way of Prevention of a
" *total Shipwrack* threatned by the
" *Adverfaries* of it, as appears fuf-
" ficiently by the Title before it,
" *viz. Propos'd in the Year* 1641. as
" an Expedient for the Prevention
" of thofe *Troubles* which afterwards
" did arife in Matters of *Church-*
" *Government, &c.* Now what can
" this, in the Senfe of any Prudent
" Unbiafs'd Perfon prejudice him in
" his Judgment or Affection to *Epi-*
" *fcopacy* it felf, which rather con-
" firms it. The *Merchant* parts
" with that in a *Storm,* that he
I 4   " would

" would not have done in a *Calm*,
" and at Shore recruits himself with
" the like Goods again. St. *Paul*
" in that Wrack, *Act.* 27. consent-
" ed not only to the lightning of the
" Ship of its Lading, but of the
" Tackling also, *We cast them out*
" (saith he, or St. *Luke*) *with our*
" *own Hands, and all for the saving*
" (if it were possible) *of the Ship,*
" *and the Passengers in it*". But now
by the way, since Archbp. *Usher's*
Judgment sways so powerfully with
you, pray comply with it in another
Particular, 'tis set down by the same
Dr. *Bernard*, in *pag.* 55. of the aforesaid Book. " For the *Form of Words*
" us'd by the *Bishop* in the *Ordina-*
" *tion* of the *Church of England*, he
" (meaning the Archbishop) did
" much approve thereof, *viz. Receive*
" *the Holy Ghost, Whose Sins thou*
" *dost remit, they are remitted, and*
" *whose Sins thou dost retain, they*
" *are retained ; and be thou a faith-*
" *ful Dispenser of the Word of God,*
and

" and of his Holy Sacraments, &c.
" And the Delivering of the *Bible*
" into the Hands of the Perſon Or-
" dain'd, ſaying, *Take thou Authority*
" *to Preach the Word of God, and Ad-*
" *miniſter the Sacraments, &c.* Which
" being wholly omitted in that of the
" *Presbyterian Way,* and no other
" *Words* to that *Senſe* us'd in their
" Room, and thereupon no expreſs
" *tranſmiſſion* of *Miniſterial Power,*
" the Archbiſhop was wont to ſay,
" *That ſuch an Impoſition of Hands*
" (by ſome call'd the *Seal* of *Ordi-*
" *nation) without a* Commiſſion *an-*
" *nex'd, ſeem'd to him to be as the*
" *putting of a* Seal *to a* Blank, *That*
" *the Scruple was not only in the* In-
" ſtrumental Cauſe, *but in the* For-
" mal: *and that if a* Biſhop *had been*
" *preſent, and done no more, the*
" *ſame Query might have been of the*
" *Validity of it*".   And in a Letter
to Dr. *Bernard,* which was publiſh-
ed, he there declar'd, " That the
" *Ordination* made by ſuch *Presby-*
                                " *ters*

" *ters,* as have fever'd themfelves
" from their *Bifhops,* unto whom
" they'd fworn *Canonical Obedience,*
" cannot be excus'd from being
" *Schifmatical (k)*". So that this
Learned Primate could find no *Sal-*
vo for our *Englifh Presbyterians,* but
he leaves them under the Guilt of
their *Schifm.* And now I fhall clofe
my Anfwer to your laft Objections,
with the Words of that Glorious
Martyr King *Charles* I. of ever Bleffed Memory, which he deliver'd in
his Difpute at *Newport* in the *Ifle of*
Wight; where that *Royal Champion*
(like another *Athanafius,* fighting
againft the World) tells thofe *Pref-*
byterian Minifters, " That he is
" not much concern'd, whether they
" call *Epifcopatus Ordo,* or *Gradus,*
" or what Name they give it, pro-
" vided they acknowledge the *Supe-*

(*k*) *This was written in his Note Book with his own Hand,
dated* 1655. *a little before his Death, as we are affur'd by
the Lord Primate's Grandfon,* James Tyrrel, *Efq; in the Ap-
pendix to his Grandfather's Life,* p. 6. *when* Epifcopacy
was at its loweft Ebb in this Ifland.

" *riority*

" *riority* of thole *Church-Officers*
" over *Presbyters* and *Deacons*".
This was formerly infinuated by that
Great and Good Prince, in his Dif-
putation with Mr. *Henderfon* at
Newcaftle, whom he routed both
Horle and Foot, and fent home that
Apoftle of the *Covenant*, a *Royal Pro-
felyte.* For this great *Athleta* (like
to the invincible *Hercules* in all his
Labours) was, in all the Difputes
that he manag'd with his unparallel-
led *Pen*, more than *Conqueror*, thro'
him that lov'd him. Yea, *Salmafius* and *Blondel* (the two great *Cham-
pions* of *Presbytery*) are conftrain'd
to grant a Difference, at leaft in the
Second Century, betwixt *Presbyters*
and *Bifhops.* And if *Blondel* from
the Year 146, (which he makes the
Epocha of that *Nominal Impropria-
tion* ;) had made a *Retrogradation* to
CXI, he would have found St. *Ignatius*, in his *Epiftles*, which are accounted *Genuine*, clearly and frequently diftinguifhing betwixt *Bifhops,*

ſhops, *Presbyters*, and *Deacons*; (and that in no leſs than thirty five ſeveral *Teſtimonies*) and theſe *Epiſtles* are now ſo fully vindicated by Archbiſhop *Uſher*, *If. Voſſius*, Dr. *Hammond* and Biſhop *Pearſon*; that all the Gratings of *Daillé*, *Salmaſius*, *Blondel*, *Capellus*, *Larroque*, and Dr. *Owen*, will never file off the leaſt Atom from their *Solidity*.

Pſeud. * *Pray*, Philalethes, *Has* Dioceſan Superiority *done any good in preventing or curing any* Schiſms ? *Has it not rather been an Occaſion (at leaſt) if not the cauſe of the Increaſe thereof ever ſince its firſt Erection? Witneſs the ſad Accounts which* Hiſtorians *and other* Eccleſiaſtical Writers *give of the many Tumults that have been rais'd, and Seditions ſtirr'd up by thoſe that Ambitiouſly ſtrove for this* Pre-eminence *and* Dignity. *Witneſs alſo thoſe frequent* Excommunications *of each other, and often-*

---

* Mr. *J. W*'s *Letters*, p. 40.

times

times for *Trifles.* *Witnefs thofe groundlefs Impofitions of Things part-ly needlefs; partly mifchievous and hurtful, on the Confciencs of* Chri-ftians, *without the leaft Warrant from* God's *Word or right Reafon, under pretence of* Decency *and* Order. *By which Lording it over* God's Heri-tage *(as* St. Peter *calls it,* 1 Pet. 5. 2.) *they have audacioufly prefum'd to exclude many from* Church-Com-munion,* *whom* Chrift Jefus *and his* Apoftles *never excluded: And that meerly for refufing to fubmit to thofe Terms, which (as they have no Rea-fon for which they fhould be urged, but the Will and Pleafure of the Im-pofers, fo) were never prefcrib'd by our* Lord.——*Hence are the Con-fciences of weak* Chriftians *infnar'd, and their Minds fill'd with perplex-ing Scruples, who ought to have been receiv'd into the* Church's Commu-nion *(if found in the Faith, and* Ho-

---

* Mr. *J. W's Letters,* p. 40, 41.

ly

ly in Life) without requiring need-less and doubtful Things as the Con-dition of that Communion, *Rom.* 14. 1, 6, 13, 15, 17, 18, 23. Hence Schifms *and* Divifions, *which have Rent the* Church *of* Chrift *and fplit it into feveral Parties, owe their Original (for the moft part) to the Impofitions of* Diocefan Pre-lacy.

Phil. Is this heavy *Charge* againft *Epifcopacy, Pfeudocheus,* laid upon the *Bifhops* of the *Romifh Church,* or upon the *Bifhops* of our *Church of England?* If 'tis laid upon the *Bifhops* of the *Romifh Church,* it does not then concern us : But if 'tis laid up-on the *Bifhops* of our *Church of Eng-land,* then you had it either from Mr. *William Prynne* of *Infamous Me-mory,* or from Mr. *Richard Baxter* of *Inveterate Malice.* If from *Prynne's Hiftory of Bifhops fince the Reformation,* then you found no-thing but *invidious Mifreprefenta-tions* and *notorious Calumnies.* And

it

if from Mr. *Baxter's Treatife of Di-*
ocefan Bifhops, his *Church Hiftory,*
or his *Plea for Peace,* then you have
nothing elfe but *abominable Stories*
taken from *Heretical Authors,* as
Philoftorgius, Sondius, and fuch o-
thers : all which are various Accounts of a great many Confufions,
rais'd by *Ambitious Presbyters,* and
their *Party,* againft the *Pious* and
Orthodox Bifhops, who fuffer'd under *Heathen, Arian,* and *Heretical*
Emperours.　　And all thofe Tranf-
actions does Mr. *Baxter* moft fhame-
fully mifapply to the *Bifhops* and
Councils; and he often fpeaks more
favourably of *Hereticks, viz.* of *A-*
rius, the *Novatians,* and the *Dona-*
tifts, who tho' they were ufurping
Presbyters, he calls them *Bifhops*;
and thro' their Sides he ftrikes at the
Sacred Office, pag. 276 of his *Plea*
for Peace. It was, *faith he, by* Bifhops *ftriving who fhould be* Chief,
that the Donatifts *fet up:* whereas
the *Donatifts* were difcontented
　　　　　　　　　　　Pref-

Presbyters. And evident it is, whatever Quarrel there was in all *Church-History,* wherein a *Bishop* was concern'd, howsoever *Innocent,* howsoever *Orthodox,* Mr. *Baxter* made him the Cause of the *Quarrel,* and was his avow'd *Adversary.* For did not Mr. *Baxter* know, (however he dissembl'd it) that *Arius* and *Aerius, Novatus* and *Novatian, Majorinus* Chaplain to *Lucilla,* a Noble Woman, with *Botruus* and *Silesius*[*], who first oppos'd *Cecilian* Bishop of *Carthage,* (and set up for *Bishops* by the Help of *Donatus,* who succeeded them, and gave Name to the *Schism*) were all of them *Presbyters?* Then afterwards they dub'd one another *Bishops,* and with whole Armies oppos'd their lawful *Bishops,* who with great Patience and Constancy withstood their Malice. And thus after the same manner, and with the like Injustice, you may

[*] *Some Writers call these* Botrus *and* Celesius.

throw

throw all the *Rebellions* and *Outra-ges*, all the *Blafphemies*, *Factions*, and *Schifms*, that have been for these Sixty Years and upwards, upon the *Bifhops* of this Realm, whereto (as 'tis very well known) the *Presbyteri-ans* first open'd the Way, and then led the Dance. Then it was, in those Times of *Violence* and *Ufurpa-tion*, (when Men did difregard their *Spiritual Guides* and *Governours*) that *Atheifm* and *Infidelity*, *Pro-fanenefs* and *Diffolutenefs of Man-ners*, and all kinds of *Difhonesty* and *Bafenefs* did Grow and Increafe. What *Difmal Tragedies* had we in that Age acted upon the Stage of our own Country? What *Bloody Wars* and *Murthers*, (*Murthers* of the *best of Kings*, and *best of Bifhops*, as alfo of *Nobles* and *Priests* ?) What *miferable Oppreffions*, *Extortions*, and *Rapines* ? What *execrable Sedi-tions* and *Rebellions* ? What *barba-rous Animofities* and *Feuds* ? What *abominable Treafons*, *Sacrileges*, *Per-*

K   *juries*

juries and *Blafphemies?* What *horrible Violations* of all *Juftice* and *Honefty?* And whence I pray was the *Source* and *Original* of all thefe Things? Did they not proceed from your *Murmurings* againft and from your *Rejecting* and *Perfecuting* your *Spiritual Governours*, from your cafting them down, from your fpurning their *Advice*, and from your trampling upon their *Authority?* Your Anceftors would have done well to have taken the Advice of St. *Ignatius*, that *Holy Martyr*, and *Difciple* of the *Apoftles*, who, in all his Epiftles to the feveral Churches, to whom he wrote, did moft earneftly prefs the *Indifpenfible Obligation* of a *ftrict Obedience* to their refpective *Bifhops*. That the *Laity* fhould fubmit themfelves to the *Presbyters* and *Deacons*, as to the *Apoftolical College* under *Chrift*; And that the *Presbyters* and *Deacons*, as well as the *Laity*, fhould Obey their *Bifhop* as *Chrift* Himfelf, whofe Perfon he did Reprefent. *For*, faith he, *as the*

Bifhop

Bishop *doth preside in the Place of*
God, *we must therefore look upon him*
as our Lord *himself ; or as our* Lord's
Representative (*l*). And that we
must be subject unto him, as unto
Jesus Christ (*m*). And that therefore whoever kept not *outward Com-*
munion with his *Bishop,* did forfeit
his *inward Communion* with *Jesus*
Christ. And 'tis not lawful without
the *Bishop,* either to *Baptize,* or *ce-*
lebrate the *Offices ;* But what he ap-
proves of, according to the good
Pleasure of *God,* that is firm and
safe, and so we do every thing se-
curely (*n*). Beware then, *Pseudo-*
cheus, of casting any *vile Aspersions*
upon the *Sacred Order* of *Episco-*
pacy: For they were *Protestant Bi-*
shops that did defend the *Reforma-*
tion by their *Writings,* and did seal
it with their *Blood.* What *Champi-*

(*l*) Προγραθμιέκ τᾶ Ἐπισκόπε εἰς τόπον Θεᾶ. Ignat. ad Mag-
nef. Τὸν ἕν Ἐπίσκοπον δῆλον ὅτι ὡς αὐτὸν ἢ Κύειον δᾶ σεςβλέπειν.
Ignat. ad Ephef. (*m*) Τῷ Ἐπ κόπῳ ὑποτασέσθι ὡς τῷ Κυείῳ.
Ignat. ad Trall. (*n*) *Ignat. ad Smyrn.*

ons

ons has the *Proteſtant Religion* ever had to be compar'd in all Reſpects with our *Cranmer, Ridley, Sands, Jewel, Parker, Bilſon, Andrews, Buckeridge, Morton, Hall, Davenant, White, Uſher, Morley, Bramhall, Gunning, Pearſon, Stillingfleet,* and many other *Biſhops* of the *Church* of *England?* And notwithſtanding the hard fortune Archbiſhop *Laud* had in other Reſpects, not to be well underſtood in the Age he liv'd in; yet his Enemies cannot deny his Book to be written with as much *Strength* and *Judgment* againſt the *Church* of *Rome,* as any other whatſoever. And had that Great and Good *Prelate* but liv'd in more *honeſt* and *better Times,* he would have been *highly Inſtrumental* in tranſmitting this *Epiſcopal Church* of *England invulnerable* to all Poſterity, by ſuch ſecure and prudent *Laws,* that no Perſon whatſoever ſhould have ever preſum'd to attempt its *Ruin.*

Then

Then *Faction* and *Sedition* would have been *chas'd* into their proper *Dens*, and sent back to inhabit those *Black* and *Dismal Regions*, where they were first invented.

And this I shall farther say of the *Bishops* of the *Church* of *England*, that they have done incomparably more *Service* against *Popery*, from the *Reformation* to this Day, than all the other *Parties* among us put together.

Pseud. *Have you done*, Philalethes?

Phil. No, Sir, your *senseless* and *indecent Reflections* upon our most excellent *Liturgy*, and our very *significant* and *useful Ceremonies* shall in the next Place fall under my Consideration. You say, * *These are* groundless Impositions *of* Things *partly* needless; *partly* mischievous *and* hurtful, *on the* Consciences *of* Christians, *without the least warrant*

---

* Mr. *J. W's Letters*, p. 40.

from

from God's Word *or* right Reaſon, *under pretence of* Decency *or* Order. To this I anſwer,

1ſt. If it be *miſchievous* and *hurtful to* the *Conſciences of Chriſtians* to uſe any thing in the *Worſhip* of God, which he himſelf has not commanded, and which is not preſcrib'd by a *Divine Law*, then what ſhall we think of the *Diſſenters* themſelves, for they uſe ſeveral Things in their *Worſhipping* of God, for which there is no *Divine Law* or *Command?* Where is it commanded that they ſhall uſe a conceiv'd *Prayer* of their own, and not *Pray* by a *Form?* Where is it commanded that they ſhould receive the *Sacrament ſitting* not *Kneeling?* Where is it commanded that the *Miniſter* ſhall be cloathed in *Black*, and ſhall not wear a *Surplice* when he *officiates?* Nay, ſeveral Things beſides that are in uſe among your *Party*, are no more expreſly commanded by a *Law* cf God, than thoſe among us.

And

And then 2dly. If it be *mischie-vous* and *hurtful* to use any thing in the *Worship* of *God*, that *God* him-self has not prescrib'd, then what shall we think of several things, that the *Jews* us'd in their *Worship*, which *God* had not commanded, and yet both our *Bleffed Saviour*, and his *Holy Apostles* comply'd with them. The ... had only a *Command* for their *Worship* in the *Temple* or in the *Tabernacle*, not in their *Synagogues*, whither our *Saviour* and his *Apostles* often reforted. The *Jews* had no *Command* in their *Law* for *reading* or *preaching Mofes* there every *Sab-bath* day, as was accuftom'd. *Act.*15. 21. Nor for that *Form* of *Prayer* and *Liturgy* which they us'd there, and in which there is no doubt, but that our *Saviour* and his *Apostles* join'd with them. There was no *Divine Command* for ... *Feaft* of the *Dedication* of the *Temple*, at which our *Saviour* was prefent, *Jo.* 10. 22. and yet he never in the leaft *repro-ved*

K 4

ved thofe appointed *Ufages*, as having any thing that was *mifchievous* and *hurtful* in them; but he comply'd with them, and countenanc'd them by his own *Example:* So alfo in the *Paffover*, which was a very confiderable *Rite* and Part of the *Jewifh Worfhip*, our *Saviour* us'd the Pofture of *Difcumbency* in the Eating of it, tho' that was not the Pofture commanded in the *Law* at the firft Inftitution of it, *Exod.* 12. 11. but it was taken up afterward by the *Jewifh Church*, when they were fettled with *Eafe* and *Liberty* in the Land of *Canaan.* And the *Cup* of *Charity* likewife, that was not of *Divine Inftitution*, yet this our *Saviour* us'd alfo after the manner of the *Jews, Luke* 22. 17. and he was pleafed to conform to many innocent and inoffenfive *Rites* of the *Jewifh Church*, in their *Divine Worfhip*, tho' they were not all of them exprefly commanded or prefcrib'd by *God.* I know, Sir, that the *Teach-ers*

ers of your *Party* do argue from
Chrift's putting an end to the *Cere-
monial Law*, that therefore they are
abfolv'd from all *Obedience* to *Ceremonies* impos'd ; and that this is their
Chriftian Liberty, to which they are
oblig'd to ftand faft, *Gal.* 5. 1. Now
at this rate, They might as well reafon from the *Abolition* of their *Judi-
cial Law* alfo, that they are freed
from their *Civil Obedience*.   Can
God be ferv'd without *Ceremony?*
And is there not a vaft Difference betwixt the *Ceremonies* of the *Jewifh*
and of our *Chriftian Church?* Thofe
were *Types* of *Chrift to come*, and to
retain them were in effect to deny
Chrift's *being come*.   And the *Liberty* St. *Paul* fpeaks of, is that of the
Gentile Chriftians, that they fhould
not fubmit to the *Jewifh Yoke*, and
has nothing at all to do in the Cafe
betwixt us.   And muft we now be
fo jealous of *Judaifm*, that becaufe
they had many *Ceremonies*, we muft
have none? According to this fort
of

of *Reafoning*, becaufe they had *Priests* and *Sabbaths*, we muft have none. For any other Offence that may be taken againft our *Rites* and *Ufages*, either as to *Multitude* or *Danger* of *Superftition*, the *Church* her felf has given that *pious* and *prudent Account* ⸏, that all, who are *pious* and *humble* themfelves, cannot but be fatisfy'd ; and truly where there is no *Humility*, I may very well queftion, whether there can be any *fincere Piety*.

And again 3dly. If it be *mifchievous* and *hurtful* to ufe any thing in the *Worfhip* of *God*, which has not been prefcrib'd in his *Holy Word*, what then fhall we think of the whole *Chriftian Church*, who did ufe fome things in their *Worfhip*, which were no way commanded by our *Saviour Chrift?* The *Salutation* of *Charity*, which is mention'd in *Rom.* 16. 16. 1 *Pet.* 5. 14. was an *outward*

⸏ *In the Preface to the* Common-Prayer-Book.

Sym-

Symbol of *Love* and *Charity*, which the *Chriſtians* us'd at their Meeting at *Prayers* and the *Sacrament*; and ſuch alſo were their *Love-Feaſts* or *Feaſts* of *Charity*, which were *Celebrated* together with the *Lord's-Supper*, 1 *Cor.* 11. 20. *Jud.* 12. Theſe and ſome others were only ſuch *Rites* as the *Chriſtians*, without any *Command* of *Chriſt*, thought fit to join with the moſt *ſolemn Parts* of the *Chriſtian Worſhip*; and yet they were of ſo indifferent and alterable a *Nature*, that the *Chriſtian Church* has thought it a Matter of *Prudence* to lay them aſide. For *God* has left ſuch *Rites* and *Ceremonies* to be determin'd by *particular Churches* and their *Governours*, and has only commanded the *Subſtantials* of his *Worſhip*, and given *general Rules* for all things to be done *decently* and in *Order* (*o*). 'Tis very plain that *God* has no where commanded them

---

(*o*) 1 *Cor.* 14. 40.

him-

himfelf, nor can there be any *particular Directory* for them produc'd out of the *Holy Scriptures*; and as plain it is that there would be perpetual *Confusion* and *Disorder* in the *Church*, if thefe were not appointed in feveral Places, by thofe who are *Governours* of it; and when they are fo commanded, if there is nothing in them, that is contrary to the *Law* of *God*, they are to be obey'd and obferv'd; they cannot be *unlawful* when no *Law* forbids them, but they may become *neceffary* in their *Ufe*, when they were *indifferent* in their *Nature*, by the *Commandment* of a *lawful Authority*; and furely there can be no *Sin* or *Superftition* in them upon that Account. Certain it is, that many Mens Diflike to our *incomparable Common-Prayers* proceeds from thofe wrong *Notions* they have of them; They think becaufe the *Roman Devotionals* retain fome part of them, that they cannot be good, becaufe
they

they have been fometimes mix'd with
what is evil : But muft we renounce
the *Holy Trinity*, and other Articles
of our *Chriftian Faith*, becaufe the
Papifts hold the fame, this would
be altogether unaccountable? The
Veffels of the *Temple* were carry'd to
Babylon, and *prophan'd* by *Belfhaz-
zar*, yet were they not *reftor'd* and
confecrated by *Ezra* to the Service of
God? There were *Liturgies* extant
in the *Church* before the *Mafs* had
either *Name* or *Being*; and *Rome
Chriftian* was much *elder* than that of
Papal: When therefore the *Myftery*
of *Iniquity* began to appear, the *Old*
or *Firft Common-Prayer* was not abolifh'd, only mix'd with *Errors* and
Corruptions; which *Blemifhes* being
now taken away, is it not as *Beauti-
ful* as ever? This then was the *pious
Care* of our *firft Reformers*, to re-
fine it from its *Drofs*, and to bring
it to its *Primitive Purity*, retaining
nothing but what is *Pure Scripture*;
or drawn therefrom by the *Judgment*

ment of our *Holy Mother* the *Church*. But we fo mightily degenerate from our *firſt Reformers*, that we will not follow thoſe *Forms*, which were pre-ſcrib'd by them ; we are for *new Lights* and *new Inventions* to guide us to *Heaven*, we deny *Common-Prayer*, and magnifie the *ſudden Raptures* of *illiterate Men*, as the *Illuminations* of the *Holy Spirit* ; when really what are they better, than an *heap of Nonſenſe* in *crampt Words*, only glaz'd over with the *Saint-like Varniſhes* of a *caſt-up Eye*, and a *canting Tone*? What *Prayers* then I pray do beſt *adorn* the *Beauty* of *Holineſs*? Thoſe, which are *ſhuf-fled* together by *Chance*, or ſuch as be *refin'd* and *poliſh'd*? Who prays moſt *believingly*, he who *digeſteth* what he prays for? Or he who *ut-ters* his *firſt Senſe* and *firſt Thoughts*? Who prays with the *fulleſt Aſſurance* to have his *Prayers heard* and *crown-ed* with *Succeſs*? He who *weighs* and *ponders* his *Petitions*? Or he who

who either by *implicit Devotion* gives
Assent to all that proceeds from the
Mouth of a *Gifted Brother*; or else
suspends his *Amen*, when he hears
things inconsistent with his *Reason*,
or the *Rule of Faith?* Thus the
Prayers of the *Church* most certainly are the best of all, and tho' we
may be allow'd in private a greater
and more *unconfin'd Freedom* of *Ex-
pression*, or with our Families in
some particular Cases, (tho' there **I**
think *Forms*, generally speaking,
most proper to be obferv'd) yet for
the *Church* of *God*, I esteem *Forms*
of *Prayer*, and an *Establish'd Liturgy*, so far from a *stinting* of the *Spirit* (as some Men would have it,
who know not what they mean, or
else would not have other poor ignorant Souls understand) that nothing
but *wild Disorder* and *Confusion*
would arife among us, if every one
(who only fancies himself *sufficient*
for the **Work**) was to be his own,
and the *Congregation's Prayer-maker*,
upon

upon every return of *Divine Worſhip,*
who knows not how to pray with the
Spirit, and to pray with the Under-
ſtanding alſo, 1 *Cor.* 14. 15. Conſider
then, *Pſeudocheus,* whence our Di-
viſions do proceed. Is it not a great
pity, that our *Bleſſed Saviour*'s *Body*
ſhould be *rent* and *torn* upon ſuch
poor Pretences? As, Whether a *Cloak*
be not more *decent* in the *Worſhip* of
God, than a *Gown* or a *Surplice?*
Whether it be not a greater *Scandal*
to *kneel* at the *Communion* with a
Papiſt, than to *ſit* or *lean* as does
their *Head* the *Pope?* Whether *ſet*
Forms of *Prayer* compos'd to the
Mind of *Holy Scripture,* have not
as fair a Claim unto the *Spirit,* as
any *unpremeditated extemporary Ef-*
fuſions? Whether the *Liturgy,* in
which the *People* bear a Part (whence
it is call'd the *Common-Prayer,* being perform'd in common by the
Flock and *Paſtor,*) be not a *Worſhip*
full as *Edifying,* as that which may
betray Men to the Surreption of
wan-

wandring Thoughts, having no *Office* to recal their roving Minds, but what concludes, the laft *Amen?* Whether it be a *Super-errogation* of *Devotion,* to fet apart and *confecrate* fome particular Days to the *Worfhip* of *God,* in which we may commemorate what was heretofore tranfacted, the *moft illuftrious Triumphs* of our *Bleffed Saviour* and his *Holy Apoftles?* Whether the *figning* of Infants with the *Crofs* in *Baptifm,* can make us more *fuperftitious* than others, whofe *Averfion* looks, as if they were afham'd of the *Crofs* of *Chrift?* Whether the *Religious Education* of Infants, may not be prudently fecur'd, by requiring Parents to provide *Sponfors* or *Sureties,* either to rebuke their Negligence if themfelves fhould be flack, or fupply their *Office,* becaufe they are Mortal? Whether *Confirmation,* the *Laying on of the Hands,* or the *Bleffing of the Bifhop,* upon the *Confeffion* of a *Novice's Faith,* be not an ad-

van-

vantagious Expedient for the *grounding* of Youth in the *Principles* of the *true Religion?* In fhort, Whether the *Communicating* with the *Primitive Chriftians* in fuch *Rites* and *Ceremonies*, as they daily pra-ctis'd, before the *See of Rome* ufurped upon the *Weftern Church*, can be a *fymbolizing* with the prefent *Papacy?* Or, if you pleafe, Whether the abufe of things themfelves moft *fignificant*, be a fufficient Reafon to reject their Ufe? Thefe, and fuch as thefe, *Pfeudochens*, are the Things which make *weak Men* fhun our *Communion*, flock into *Conventicles*, and divide into *Factions*: Thefe were the *Beginnings* of that *Breach*, which is now grown up into an open and moft dreadful *Schifm*: And is the *Peace* of the *Church* fo meer a Cypher, that Men are lefs tender of it, than tenacious of their own *Opinions?* But *Scruples* and *Diffentions* will arife, fo long as Men are fir'd from below, and fo wretchedly deluded

luded and infatuated by the *Prince of Darkness.* How fuccefsful has that *evil Spirit* been in *fomenting* our *Enmities* and *heightning* our *Animofities?* Was it not he who caus'd the *Schifm* of *Corah, Dathan* and *Abiram?* Did not he caufe the *Separation* of the *Euftachians?* Was it not he who kindled that *Schifmatical* Fire of the *Donatifts?* Did not he blow it up into fuch *difmal* and *raging Flames,* that they had almoft *burnt* and *confum'd* the whole *Church,* yea even turn'd it into *Afhes,* had not that *Council* in *Africa* been Affembl'd to *quench* and *allay* its *Fury?* And tell me, I befeech you, are not thefe *Embers* afrefh reviv'd? If we reflect on thofe, who at this very Day, difturb the *Peace* of our *Jerufalem,* we fhall find them to be of the fame *Dye* and *Complexion,* herein only differing, that thofe of this Age have fcrap'd the *fhreds* of all *old* and *outworn Heterodoxies,* to patch them up in a *Scotch* or *Geneva Garb.* L 2 Where-

Wherefore, *Pseudocheus*, let every one of us, with bended Knees and lift up Hands, intreat the *Holy God*, that he would be pleas'd to pity the *Vine*, that his own *Right Hand* hath planted, that the *Catholick Church* may be so guided and govern'd by his *good Spirit*, that all who profess and call themselves *Christians*, may be led into the way of *Truth*, and hold the *Faith* in *Unity* of *Spirit*, in the *Bond* of *Peace*, and in *Righteousness* of *Life*.

Pseud. *Indeed*, Philalethes, *you have largely consider'd most of my Arguments against* Diocesan Episcopacy, *but some others there are that you have pass'd by, without any manner of regard; Pray, Sir, let me know what you mean by your so doing, and what also you have to say to this very Argument among the rest ? If there must be* Diocesan Bishops *to prevent* Schism *among the* Presbyters, *then there must be* Archbishops *to prevent* Schism *among the* Bishops;
and

and then Patriarchs *to govern* Archbifhops; *and laftly,* a Pope *to pre-*
vent Schifm *among the* Patriarchs.
And thus by your profound Reafon-
ing, the Papacy *will be Eftablifh'd o-*
ver the whole Chriftian *World, by*
Vertue of the fame Neceffity which is
pleaded for a Bifhop *over his* Diocefe.

Phil. I have confider'd, Sir, all
your *Doughty Arguments,* and have
fufficiently difprov'd them; and as
for the others (you fpeak of) that
are omitted, they are fo *weak,* fo
trifling and fo *illogical,* that they do
not deferve any ferious *Confutation*;
yet to oblige you a little in your
Requeft, be pleas'd to fee what *John*
Calvin faith to your laft Argument.
You'll find it in the *1ft* and *4th Secti-*
ons of the *4th Chap.* of his *Inftituti-*
ons: His Words are thefe : `` As we
`` have fhown there is a *threefold*
`` *Miniftry* commended to us in
`` *Scripture*; So whatever *Minifters*
`` the *Ancient Church* had, it diftin-
L 3 `` guifh'd

" guish'd them into *Three Orders*,
" *Bishops, Presbyters* and *Deacons*".
And §. 4. " That every *Province*
" had among their *Bishops*, one who
" was an *Archbishop*, and that in
" the *Council* of *Nice*, *Patriarchs*
" were appointed, who in *Order*
" and *Dignity* might be *Superior* to
" *Archbishops*, This was for Prefer-
" vation of *Discipline*, that if any
" thing hapned in any *Church* which
" could not well be determin'd by a
" few, it might be referr'd to a *Pro-*
" *vincial Synod*, and if the Affair
" was of such Importance that it re-
" quir'd a greater Discussion, Ap-
" plication was made to the *Patri-*
" *arch* with the *Synods*, from whom
" there was no Appeal, but to a
" *General Council*". And faith he
a little farther in the same *Section*,
" We shall find that the *Ancient Bi-*
" *shops* had no mind to frame any o-
" ther *Form* of *Church Government*,
" than what was prescrib'd by *God*
" in his *Word*.

But

But, Sir, there are some other
sort of Arguments, which you have
so peculiarly manag'd, that you seem
to be alike Skilful in *Logick*, as heretofore I once observ'd you in *Natural Philosophy*, when I heard you
say, *That our* Cold Summers *were
caus'd by the late* Earthquake*, which
had remov'd the Earth* 15 Degrees
towards the North-Pole.

Pseud. *You may represent me as you
please, but methinks you might have
had a greater Respect for the Me-
mory of our late* Pious *and* Precious
Friend Mr. Richard Baxter, *than to
charge such an* Holy Man *with the*
Guilt *of so many* Crimes. *What say
you to this,* Philalethes?

Phil. This I say, *Pseudocheus,* that
a great Part of the *Venom* you have
discharg'd upon the *Church of England,* you before imbib'd from Mr.
Baxter's *virulent Principles.* You
say, *That the* Schisms *and* Divisions

---

* *This* Earthquake *happen'd in the Year,* 1693

L 4   *which*

which have Rent the Church of Chrift *, *and Split it into feveral* Parties, *owe their Original (for the moft Part) to the Impofitions of Diocefan Prelacy.* Now this is all over Mr. *Baxter.* But if you had confulted the Hiftories of *Ecclefiaftical Feuds* and *Tumults*, or thofe *Schifms* occafion'd by *Novatus* and the *Donatifts*, you would have found it a very difficult Task to prove any *lawful Bifhop* to have been the *Founder* of any of thofe *Schifms* and *Divifions* which you fpeak of. And it may be with fome fort of Reafon faid of you, what Mr. *Herle* (*p*), a noted *Presbyterian* faid of Mr. *Baxter*, as your own Mr. *Bagfhaw* reports; *That it had been happy for the Church of* God, *if Mr.* Baxter's *Friends had never fent him to School.* Of which Opinion was Mr. *Cawdry* alfo, who was another of his own

---

Mr. *J. W's Letters*, p 41.　(*p*) *Mr.* Herle *was* Prolocutor *to the* Affembly *of* Divines, *and Rector of* Winwick *in* Lancafhire *in the Time of the* Great Rebellion.

Fra-

Fraternity. Then fee what *Chara-* *&er* Mr. *Baxter* is pleas'd to give of himfelf, in his Letter to Dr. *Hill.* *I have been,* faith he, *in the Heat of my Zeal fo forward to* Changes *and* Ways of Blood, *that I fear* God *will not let me have a Hand in the peaceable Building of his Church.* We commonly fay, *Pfeudocheus, De Mortuis nil nifi bene,* That we ought to fay nothing but well of the Dead; Yet when Men have been *notorioufly wicked* in their *Principles* and *Practices,* they fhould then be *expos'd,* that others may *abominate* and *detest* thofe *flagrant Villanies ,* that fuch have been guilty of, and of which, as 'tis very well known, Mr. *Baxter* himfelf was not wholly *innocent.* Do but take this one Inftance, as 'tis related by Mr. *Vernon,* in the Clofe of his *Preface* to Dr. *Heylin*'s *Life.*

" Mr. *Baxter* (fays he) may be
" pleas'd to call to mind what was
" done to Old Major *Jennings,* in
" the laft War, in the Fight that was
" he-

" between *Linfel* and *Longford* in
" *Salop* ; where the *King's Party*
" being worfted, the Major was ftript
" almoft Naked, and left for Dead
" in the Field : But Mr. *Baxter* and
" one Lieutenant *Hurdman* walking
" among the wounded and dead Bo-
" dies, perceiv'd fome Life left in
" the Major, and *Hurdman* run him
" thro' the Body in cold Blood, Mr.
" *Baxter* all the while looking on,
" and taking off with his own Hand
" the *King's* Picture from about his
" Neck, telling him as he was fwim-
" ming in his Gore, that he was a *Po-*
" *pifh* Rogue, and that was his *Cruci-*
" *fix :* which Picture was kept by Mr.
" *Baxter* for many Years, till it was
" got from him, but not without
" much difficulty, by one Mr. *Sum-*
" *merfield,* who then liv'd with Sir
" *Thomas Rous,* and generoufly re-
" ftor'd it to the poor Man now alive
" at *Wiche* near *Parfhore* in *Worce-*
" *fterfhire,* altho' at the Fight fup-
" pos'd to be dead, being after the
" Wounds

" Wounds given him, dragg'd up and
" down the Field by the merciless
" Soldiers ; Mr. *Baxter* approving
" of the *Inhumanity*, by *feeding* his
" Eyes with so *bloody* and *barbarous*
" a *Spectacle*. For the Truth of
" which we have this *Subscription*.

I Thomas Jennings *subscribe to
the Truth of this Narrative above-
mention'd, and have hereunto put my
Hand and Seal the Second Day of*
March, 168¼. *Sign'd and Seal'd in
the presence of*

John Clerk, *Minister of* Wiche,
Tho. Darke.

Pseud. *Enough, enough,* Philalethes, *Let all his Imperfections be bu-
ried with him in his Grave, Earth to
Earth, Ashes to Ashes, Dust to Dust.*

Phil. I knew you would not pro-
ceed any farther according to the
Form us'd in the *Church* of *England.*
What, have you not a Hope of your
Friend's *Resurrection* to *Eternal
Life?* It may be you have heard as
much

much of Mr. *Baxter* as the Learned and Ingenious Mr. *Long* of *Excefter* has recorded of him in this *Chara-Eteriftical Epitaph.*

Hic jacet RICHARDUS BAXTER,
Theologus Armatus,
Loiolita Reformatus,
Hærefiarcha Ærianus,
Schifmaticorum Antifignanus :
Cujus pruritus difputandi peperit,
Scriptitandi Cacoethes nutrivit,
Prædicandi zelus intemperatus maturavit,
ECCLESIÆ SCABIEM :
Qui diffentit ab iis quibufcum-confentit maximè,
Tum fibi cùm aliis Nonconformis
Præteritis, præfentibus, & futuris :
Regum & Epifcoporum Juratus Hoftis,
Ipfumq; Rebellium Solenne Fœdus :
Qui natus erat per Septuaginta Annos,
Et Octoginta Libros :
Ad perturbandas Regni Refpublicas,
Et ad bis perdendam Ecclefiam Anglicanam :
Magnis tamen excidit Aufis,
Deo Gratias.

And fo much for your precious Mr. *Baxter.*

Pfeud.

Pseud. *I am very glad you have
done with* Mr. Baxter, *for I had almost
forgotten, what I have just now re-
collected. Pray tell me what you
think of the* French *and* Scotch *Churches? Was there not more Union and
Concord, and less Errors and Heresies among them, before the Introdu-
ction of* Prelacy *than in any* Prelatical Church *in the World* * *? And yet
both these renounc'd all* Subordination *to* Bishops *as to a* Superior Office,
nor could ever acknowledge their Divine Right.

Phil. How now! Sir. Shall we
never have done with Mr. *Baxter?*
This you had from his *Treatise of
Episcopacy* †, where he saith, " The
" *Church of Scotland* is an Eminent
" Instance, that *Churches* which have
" no *Bishops* have incomparably less
" *Heresie, Schism, Wickedness,* and
" more *Concord* than we have". Now
how contrary are these Thoughts to

---

* Mr. *J. W's Letters,* p. 41. † *Treatise of Episcopacy,*
p. 1. p. 164.

those

thole of the moſt Worthy Men of the *Foreign Churches*, who were no *Oppoſers*, but *Approvers of Epiſcopal Order* and *Government* for the prevention of *Errors* and *Hereſies*, as has been ſufficiently ſhew'd by many Principal Perſons among them? And even in the *Synod of Dort*, when thoſe ſent from *England* aſſerted *Episcopacy as Apoſtolical*, there was not (as they declar'd in their joint *Atteſlation*) any one Perſon in that *Synod* who ſpake a Word againſt it, and as Bp *Hall* acquaints us, The *Preſident* of the *Synod* ſaid*, *Domine, non licet nobis eſſe tam felices:* We may not be ſuch happy Men (*q*). And firſt, As for the *French Churches,* they were ſeveral times in great Danger of being Rent in Pieces, by the many *Feuds* and *Diſſentions,* which daily aroſe among them , had not the Great and the Good *Du-Pleſſis* by his Learning and Prudence

---

* Johannes Bogermannus *Miniſter of* Lewarden.
(*q*) *Bp* Hall's *Divine Right of Epiſcopacy, p nt. c. 4.*

ery

very frequently appeas'd their *Ani-mofities*, and put an End to their *Controverfies.* " But after his Death, " the *Peace* of thofe *Churches* was " very much endanger'd by a New " *Controverfie* about *Univerfal Re-* " *demption*, and the Nature of *Ori-* " *ginal Sin :* and the *Diffention* was " not far from a *Schifm. Cameron*, " tho' he had clear'd himfelf of all " Sufpicion of *Heterodoxy* at his " Promotion to the *Profefforfhip* of " *Saumur*, was fo unfortunate after- " wards to be fufpected of *Herefie :* " and his Pupils and Followers were " not a little perplex'd. What had " been approv'd by the *Synod of* " *Dort*, as *Orthodox* Doctrine in the " *Englifh Divines*, was now call'd " into Queftion in *France ;* and " what was allow'd in *Cameron* " while he was alive, was *Heretical* " and pernicious after his Death *. " It is hardly to be imagin'd (faith

* *Acts Authentiques, per Blondel.*

" my

" my Author) what great *Conten-*
" *tion* this little, and to fome, im-
", perceptible *Difference* did create;
" or how many *Synods* it imploy'd,
" *Amyraldus, Daillé, Blondel,* and
" feveral others were look'd upon
" as little better than *Hereticks*, and
" their *Doctrine* about *Original Sin*
" Condemn'd in a *National Synod*
" at *Charenton,* and an *Abjuration*
" of it requir'd of all thofe that were
" to enter into *Holy Orders*; and a
" ftrict *Injunction* was laid on all
" *Minifters,* upon Pain of all the
" *Cenfures* of the *Church,* not to
" Preach any otherwife of this *Point,*
" than according to the *Common O-*
" *pinion.* And all this Stir, as *Blon-*
" *del, (p. 50.)* deduces it, was rai-
" fed from little Private Quarrels
" between fome of the *Profeffors*;
" and from the *Difcontents* of the
" *Univerfity* of *Montauban,* that they
" of *Saumur* fhould be favour'd too
" much in the Diftribution of fuch
" *Penfions* as the *Churches* furnifh-
" ed

" ed for the Maintenance of their
" *Univerſities* ; and they thought
" themſelves wrong'd and underva-
" lu'd, becauſe their Salaries were
" leſs : Thus we ſee that leſſer Mat-
" ters than a *Biſhoprick* can ſome-
" times diſturb the *Peace* of the
" *Church* , and that *Presbyters*, as
" well as *Biſhops*, can proſecute their
" *Private Quarrels* to the hurt of
" the *Publick Peace* , and that there
" will be *Errors, Contentions*, and
" *Animoſities* where there is no *Epi-*
" *ſcopacy.*

And then 2dly. The *Concord* of
the *Church* of *Scotland*, was much
greater while it continu'd under *Bi-*
ſhops, than it has been ſince *Andrew*
Melvil inflam'd it with the *General*
Government and *Diſcipline*. And becauſe you would perſwade us, that
there has been more *Union* and *Con-*
cord in this *Scotch Anti-Epiſcopal*
Church, than in the *Epiſcopal Church*
of *England* ; I will give you one Inſtance, that you may ſee how far this

M   Way

is from *Establishing* an *Union* and
Concord; and that this *Parity* here
pretended, is no other than a *meer
Pretence*, the *Leading-Men* against
Bishops commonly assuming a greater
Authority, and exercising it with
greater *Absoluteness*, and are more
Impatient of being oppos'd and contradicted, than any *Bishops* who are
legally Trusted with *Power*.

" There happen'd a great *Divi-*
" *sion* in the *Presbytery* of St. *An-*
" *drews*, about preferring a Minister
" to the Church of *Luchars*. There
" were two Pretenders, and *Melvil*
" with a few more was for one, and
" the Rest, who were three times as
" many in Number, were for the
" other; *Melvil* looking upon him-
" self as an *Apostle*, and disdaining
" to be over-rul'd by the Majority
" of the *Presbytery*, left the Place,
" and with his six *Presbyters* that
" follow'd him, made another *Synod*

---

* Spottiswood's *Hist.* of Scotland.

" by

" by himſelf: and both theſe *Presby-*
" *ters*, like *Anti-Popes*, iſſu'd out their
" ſeveral Pleaſures. The Gentlemen
" of the *Pariſh* upon this were divi-
" ded into *Factions*, ſome holding
" with one, and ſome with the o-
" ther, which occ ſion'd great Scan-
" dal: and the *Heats* grew to that
" Height, that the *Presbytery* was
" forc'd to be divided; one Part of
" it to ſit at St. *Andrews*, the other
" at *Cowper*, the one under the In-
" fluence of *Melvil*, and the other
" under that of *Thomas Buchanan*;
" ſo hard it was for one *Presbyterial*
" *Dioceſe* to hold two *Topping Preſ-*
" *byters*". The Obſervation upon
this in *Spotſwood* (*p*. 386.) is very
remarkable. " Thus was that great
" Strife pacify'd, which many held
" to be Ominous; and that the *Go-*
" *vernment* which in the Beginning
" did break forth into ſuch *Schiſms*,
" could not long continue; for this
" every Man noted, That of all Men
" none could worſe endure *Parity*,

" and

" and lov'd more to *Command*, than
" they who had introduc'd it into
" the *Church*. This fort of Men did
" afterwards make not only a *Formal*
" *Schifm*, and *Infurrection* againſt
" thofe *Biſhops* plac'd over them by
" *Authority*, but after that Epiſco-
" pacy was Abolifh'd in *Scotland*,
" could be as little at *Peace* among
" themſelves. They were in the firſt
" place divided about receiving the
" *King*, and the *Conditions* to be im-
" pos'd upon him ; and in this they
" proceeded even to the *Excommuni-*
" *cation* of one another. After his
" *Majeſty's Reſtauration*, when Epi-
" fcopacy was Eſtablifh'd again in
" the *Church*, the *Presbyterians*
" who fepuated from the *Communi-*
" *on* of the *Biſhops*, were divided
" yet among themſelves, ſome ac-
" cepting the *King's Indulgence* and
" *Licence* to *Preach*, others *renoun-*
" *cing* it as derogatory to the *King-*
" *dom* of *Jeſus Chriſt*, and upon this
" they parted *Communion* : Nor cou'd
" theſe

" thele *Refolute Renouncers* of *In-*
" *dulgence* agree yet among them-
" felves, about the meafure of their
" *Contempt* of *Authority*; fome were
" content to *Conventicle*, and Preach
" againft the *King's Order*, and car-
" ry their *Contempt* no farther, the
" others under *Cameron* were more
" *fiercely zealous*, and thought them-
" felves oblig'd by the *Covenant* to
" attempt the *Depofing* of the *king*, as
" they manifefted (befides their fe-
" veral *Writings* to that effect) by
" two *Formal Rebellions*. Thele are
" the *Fruits*, this the *Peace*, *Unity*,
" and *Concord* that *Presbytery* hath
" produc'd". And truly after all,
to judge of things impartially, without Prejudice or Paffion, *Epifcopacy*
feems not only the moft *Ancient*, but
the moft *Natural Government* of the
Church, and we may obferve in the
manifold *Revolutions* and *Changes* of
the *Church* of *Scotland*, and the different *Schemes* of *Government* introduc'd in that Nation, which were

M 3 found

found *violent* and *burthensome*, so
that the People would not bear them
long, their *final* and *common Refuge*
was *Episcopacy*, as the suitable and
proper Government thereby to recover their Breach.

This you see, *Pseudocheus*, that
in the *French* and *Scotch Churches*
there has not been that *Union* and
Concord, which has been in our *Episcopal Church* of *England*, and tho'
you say also that there has been less
Heresies Errors and in those *Churches* than in any *Prelatical Church*
whatsoever; yet I must needs tell you,
that there were never any *Hereticks* in
the World, but what were likewise
Anti-Episcopal; and at the same
time they began in *Schism*, and became Enemies to Truth, they decla-
red War against the *Bishops*, who were
the *Guardians* of it, and so ended
in *Enthusiasm* and *Madness*. Some
of them were first *Presbyterians*, and
when that *Dispensation* was not *Spiritual* enough, they then Improv'd
into

into *Independents*, and from thence turn'd into *Quakerism*. So that all the *Extravagant Heresies* among us are but the *Spawns* of the *first Schism*, and the Consequences of those *Principles* of *Separation*, that draw them from the *Communion* of the *Bishop*.

Pseud. *Well, Sir, here are two more Questions for you, and then I have done. The first is, "Why do you not admit the* French *and* Dutch *Protestant Ministers to the Cures of Souls in this Kingdom (tho' never so Learned, and willing to comply with you in all other things) without submitting to* Re-Ordination *by a* Bishop, *When at the same time you admit a* Popish-Priest, *that turns* Protestant, *without any* New Ordination, *because he was* Ordain'd *by a* Bishop, *altho' a* Popish *one ?* You plainly thereby declare, what the Tendency of your Doctrine is.

Phil. The Nine and thirty Articles of our Religion, and the Statute Laws of

the Realm will not permit any *Foreign Protestant Minister* to have a
Cure of Souls in this Kingdom without *Episcopal Ordination*: But a *Popish Priest* that turns *Protestant*, has
no more need of *Re-Ordination*, than
Archbishop *Cranmer* had of *Re-Con-
secration*, after he had been *Confecrated* by three *Popish Bishops* upon
the 30th. of *March*, 1533. in the
24th. of *Henry VIII.* *, who were
John Longland, Lord Bishop of *Lin-
coln*, *John Voysey*, Lord Bishop of
Exeter, and *Henry Standish*, Lord
Bishop of St. *Asaph.* And the Reason of this is very plain, because the
Church of Rome is a *true Church*, so
far as it agrees with *Truth*; and tho'
it is *Idolatrous* and wonderfully cor-
rupted in its *Principles*, yet its *Ido-
latries* and *Corruptions* has no more
Un-Church'd it, than *Aaron's Idola-
try Un-Priested* him, for he continu'd the *High-Priest* still. Here eve-

* *See* Mason's *Confecration of Bishops in the Church of* England, p. 66.

ry

ry Body may plainly fee the Tendency of your *Learning* and *Judgment*.

Pfeud. *This is more than I have heard before, and therefore I shall not give you any farther trouble upon that Head, but will now proceed to my last Question. How do you know that you was* lawfully Ordain'd ? * *He that* Ordain'd *you must have been a* Bifhop rightly Ordain'd *by another* Bifhop; *(if not Three) and He by a Third* †; *and fo to the very* Apoftles *in an uninterrupted Succeffion of* true Bifhops: *Elfe you are no* true Minifter. *For the least Interruption or Failure in this Succeffion does, according to you, cause a meer Nullity. Then you must either Recant your odd Notion, or be forc'd (if you would be Confiftent with your felf) to turn* Seeker. *Now tell me, if you can, whether fuch a* Succeffion *as this be poffible to be prov'd?*

---

* *Mr. J. W's Letters*, p. 53.   † Pfeudocheus *means* Three others.

Phil.

Phil. The *Church of England* has those *indubitable Records* to prove the *Consecrations* and *uninterrupted Successions* of her *Bishops*, that any *Clergyman* finding out that *Bishop*, that gave him *Orders*, may ascend in a *Right Line* of *Bishops*, even to the Time of the *Holy Apostles.* And the Truth of this is so very obvious to any Person, who has consulted our *Ecclesiastical Histories*, that I have no manner of Reason to recant my *Notions* in these Matters, or to seek for any farther *Character* of your *Qualifications*, because I am very well assur'd, that your *Ignorance* in *Church-Affairs* does most wretchedly betray you into many gross and unaccountable *Errors.*

And now after all, if you will permit your self to weigh and consider the foregoing *Testimonies* and *Arguments*, which I have here produc'd for the *Establishment* and *Confirmation* of *Diocesan Episcopacy*, I do not perceive how you can deny it to have been

been practis'd in the *Apostolical Age*,
without destroying the very *Faith* of
the *Primitive Church*, without weak-
ning that *Testimony* on which we receive the *Canon* of the *New Testament*
in a Matter as *Notorious*, as that *Canon* it self. " Not to mention the
" *Testimony* of *Ignatius*, faith the
" very Judicious and Learned Mr.
" *Dodwel* (*r*), tho' truly I think
" they who question it, (since the
" late excellent Defence of it perfor-
" med with as great Evidence as a
" Matter of that *Antiquity* (*s*), af-
" ter the miscarriage of so many
" *Primitive Records*, is capable of)
" might as well have question'd se-
" veral Books of the *New Testament*
" it self, which notwithstanding
" they receive on lesser Evidence ; I
" say, not to mention this, What
" can they say to the **Angels** in the
" *Revelations*? What to the *Testimo-
" ny* of St. *Irenæus* concerning St.

(*r*) *See Mr* Dodwell*s Separation of Churches, &c. ch.*
24. § viii, *& ix.* (*s*) *In vindic. Ig* *nt, cont. Dalen n.*

" *Poly-*

" *Polycarp,* who feems to have been
" one of them, whom he makes to
" have been *Ordain'd Bishop* of
" *Smyrna* by the *Apoflles* themfelves
" (*t*) ? What to the *Teftimony* of
" *Clemens Alexandrinus* who men-
" tions *Bishops* among other *Offices*
" of the *Church* fettled by St. *John*
" (*u*) ? What to the *Teftimony* of
" *Hegefippus,* who makes the Kinf-
" men of our *Saviour* to have been
" made *Bishops* from *Domitian's*
" time to that of *Trajan* (*w*) ?
" What to thofe who mention St.
" *James* to have been made *Bishop*
" of *Jerufalem* by the *Apoflles* them-
" felves (*x*) ? What of the *Seven*
" *Polycrates* mentions as *Bishops* in
" his own See before himfelf, the
" firft of which feems, in all likeli-
" hood, to have begun in the *Apo-*
" *flles* times (*y*) " Nay, what to

(*t*) *Iren. l.* 3. *adv. Harif. & apud Euf. Hift.* 4. 14·
(*u*) *Clem. Alexand.* ἧς ὁ πλειοσοῶς *apud Euf. Hift.* 3. 23·
(*w*) *Euf. l.* 3 *Hift. Eccl. c.* 20. (*x*) *Euf. Hift.* 2. 1·
(*y*) *Euf. Hift.* 5. 24·

all

" all thofe Catalogues of *Bifhops* fuc-
" ceeding in the four *Patriarchal*
" *Sees*, particularly the fifteen in
" *Jerufalem*, from St. *James* to the
" Deftruction of the *Jews* under *A-*
" *drian* (*z*)? Nay, what to the
" *Succeffion* of all the *Apoftolical Sees*
" to which the *Fathers* of the *Second*
" *Century* do fo folemnly appeal to
" prove their own *Doctrine Apofto-*
" *lical* in oppofition to the contra-
" ry Pretences of the *Hereticks* (*a*)?
" Can they think them all to have
" been either *wilful Forgeries*, or
" *general Miftakes* in a *Matter* of
" *Fact* fo near their own time, with-
" out fo much as any likely ground
" in *Hiftory?* How will they then
" affure us, that they were not mi-
" ftaken in delivering to us the *Books*
" of the *Apoftles*, which were not
" more *Notorious* to them than their
" *Government*". And this *Line* of
Apoftolical Succeffion of *Bifhops* has

(*z*) *Euf Hift* 4 5   (*a*) *Tertull Præfc. hæn adverf.*
Hæref.

con-

continu'd thro' all Ages of the *Church*
to our prefent Times, and no other
Government than what was *Epifco-*
pal, was ever heard of in the World,
for the Space of 1500 Years. So that
he who is out of this Line of *Apo-*
ftolical Succeffion, and exercifes any
Miniſterial Office without the *Com-*
miffion of *Epifcopal Ordination,* is
but a *Lay-Impoſtor* and a *Schifma-*
tick from the *Catholick Church.* And
all other *Societies* of *Chriſtian* People,
who totally withdraw themſelves
from the *Government* of their *Biſhops,*
who are the *Holy Apoſtles Succeſſors,*
and from the *Miniſtry* of thofe *Pref-*
byters lawfully ſet over them by E*pi-*
fcopal Ordination and *Inſtitution,*
and do caſt themſelves into any o-
ther *Model* of *Government,* are all of
them Guilty of *Schifm.* And now
to ſhew the *deteſtable Wickednefs* of
your *Uſurpation,* it will be here very
neceſſary to take a ſmall View of the
Dignity of our *Prieſtly Office,* which
you and others of your Fraternity
have

have fo audacioufly prefum'd to invade. St. *Chryfoftom* in his Difcourfe Πεзὶ Ἱεεϲούνϛ, concerning the *Priest-hood*, does highly magnifie the *Office* and *Authority* of a *Priest*, He there tells us, Ἱξϱϭίαν ἔλαξει ὡ ἔτε Ἀγγέλοις ὅτε Ἀρχαγγέλοις ἔδωϰεν ὁ Θεὸν, *&c.* That *God* has invefted the *Priest* with fuch *Authority*, as he never conferr'd upon *Angels* or *Arch-Angels.* For to which of the *Angels* did he fay at any time, *Whatever ye bind on Earth is bound in Heaven ; and whofe Sins ye Remit, they are Remitted ?* For as the Father gave Power to the Son to remit Sins, fo the Son of *God* hath committed the fame Power to his Minifters on Earth.

The *Office* of the *Magiftrate* (fays Bp. *Moffom*) intends the *Eftablifh-ment* of *Peace* ; the *Art* of the *Phy-fician*, the *Health* of the *Body* ; the *Profeffion* of the *Lawyer*, the *Securi-ty* of the *Eftate* ; but the *Calling* of the *Minifter*, the *Salvation* of the *Soul :* Which *Sacred Office*, however
flighted

flighted by Men, yet 'tis Honour'd and Efteem'd of *God*, and 'tis call'd by the *Holy Apoftle* an *excellent Work*, I *Tim.* 3. 1. And this is fome Part of its *Excellency*; that the *Minifter* in *Publick Prayer* is the Peoples *Mouth*, as their *Orator* unto God; and in *Publick Preaching*, he is *God's Mouth*, as his *Ambaffador* unto the People, and thus what Honour can be greater than this, to have Ψυχῶν προστασίαν ἢ μεσιτείαν Θεῶ ἢ Ἀνθρώπων (as St. *Gregory Nazianzen* fpeaks *) a *Prefidentfhip* of *Souls*, and a kind of *Mediatorfhip* 'twixt *God* and *Men?* Obferve then the *Minifter* at the *Altar*, and I will not fay, What *Prince* on his *Throne?* but what *Seraphim* in *Heaven*, is imployed in a Service of more *Dignity* and *Honour* than this, to offer unto God the *Commemorative Sacrifice* of his *Son's Body* and *Blood?*

And now from the *Dignity* of the *Minifterial Office*, is aggravated the

* *Nazianz. Apolog.*

Guilt

Guilt of their *Usurpation*, who pre-
sume to exercise any proper *Ministe-
rial Power* in the Name of *God* or
Christ, without sufficient *Authority*.
The severe Punishment of *Saul*'s *Sa-
crificing*, by the Loss of his *Kingdom*,
1 *Sam.* 13. 13, 14. and of *Uzziah*'s
offering Incense, by his being smit-
ten with *Leprosie*, which rendred
him uncapable not only of *Governing* the *Kingdom*, but of having *Society* with the *Congregation* of the
Lord, 2 *Chron.* 26. 19, 21. testifie
how much *God* was provok'd thereby. The *dreadful Judgment* upon
Corah and his Company, for *offering Incense*, and pleading the *Right*
of all the *Congregation* of *Israel* a-
gainst *Moses* and *Aaron*, as if they had
taken too much upon them, was very remarkable. And much more is it
sinful and *dangerous* to intrench upon the *Office* of the *Gospel-Ministry*:
because the *Institution* of *Christ*, the
Authority convey'd by him, and the
Grace conferr'd from him, are things

N   more

more *sublime* and *sacred*, than what was deliver'd by *Moses*. Can you then think that *God* was more jealous for the *Legal*, than he is for the *Evangelical Ministration?* Did he punish *Kings* invading the *Office* of the *Priest*, and will he acquit the *People* usurping the *Function* of the *Minister?* No certainly; for we must know, that under the *Law*, *God*'s *Judgments* and *Blessings* were generally *corporal* and *temporal*, but under the *Holy Gospel*, they are generally *spiritual* and *eternal*; so that, to be given up to a *Blindness* of *Mind*, and a *Reprobate Sense*, seems to be a *Judgment* upon all *Fanaticks*, and the most *dreadful Vengeance* that can befal any sort of People.

And now after all, since *Episcopal Ordination* has been of so general Practice, from the time of the *Apostles* in the *Church* of God, and is regularly Establish'd and continu'd in this Kingdom; no Man in this *Church*, with Respect to *Order*, *U-nity*

nity and *Apoſtolical Inſtitution*, can reaſonably expect that *God* will ever own him as his *Officer* in the *Miniſtry* of *Reconciliation*, unleſs he be admitted thereto by ſuch *Ordination*. And Private *Chriſtians* both out of *Duty* to *God*, and out of *Reſpect* to their own *Safety*, ought to avoid and ſhun all you *counterfeit* and *pretended Miniſters*, who do oppoſe your ſelves againſt this *Sacred Order*, becauſe of the Danger under the *New Teſtament* of periſhing in the Gain-ſaying of *Core*, *Jude*, *v.* 11. And here we may obſerve, that *Corah* and his *confederate Mutineers* were neither *Hereticks* nor *Apoſtates*, but Men of the ſame *Creed* with *Moſes* and *Aaron*: their *Crime* was the *Violating* that *Subordination* which *God* had appointed, and not ſubmitting themſelves to the *Superior Authority* of the *Prieſthood*. So that hereupon *God* was then pleas'd to puniſh one *Schiſm* with another, For *The*

N 2 * *Earth*

* *Earth open'd and swallow'd up Dathan, and cover'd the Company of Abiram,* Psal. 106. 17. As for the *Reasons* which the *Dissenters* produce to justifie their *desperate Schism,* they have been so frequently and fully answer'd, that 'tis a Wonder they have not return'd generally into the *Bosom* of the *Church,* if it were not a greater, how they could ever break the *Unity* of it for such *Reasons.* For, among all the *Divisions* that have infested the *Church* of *God,* none ever began a *Schism* about the *External Rites* of *Religion,* except our *Dissenters* in *England,* who for the very same *Reasons* that they have *separated* from this *Church,* must have *separated* from the *Primitive Church,* which observ'd more *Rites* than ours; and if even the *Primitive Church* was not *Holy* and *Pure* enough for them to *Communicate* with, let them consider what be-

---

* Num. 16. v. 31. *The Ground clave asunder—* ——

comes

comes of two Articles of the r Creed, *The Holy Catholick Church,* and the *Communion of Saints.*

How c[...]l was our *Blessed Saviour* in the training up of his *Holy Apostles,* and what Pains did he take with them, that they might be thoroughly instructed, and not differ in the Delivery of his Mind to the World, and with what *extraordinary Ardor* (*Joh.* 17. 11.) he pray'd for them upon this very Account? And then with what *Diligence* and *Circumspection* did the *Holy Apostles* answer their *Master's Care?* How industrious were they to resist all the *beginnings* of *Schism* in every *Church,* to heal the *Breaches,* to take away all occasions of *Division,* to unite all *Hearts,* and to reconcile all *Minds?* How did they instruct the People to abominate this *Distemper* as the *Bane* of *Christianity,* charging them to avoid all Men that inclin'd that Way, as Persons of a *Contagious Breath* and *Infectious Society?* What *detestable*

N 3 *Names*

Names they gave to *Schism* in those Days, as *Carnality, the Work of the Flesh, and of the Devil?* 1 *Cor.* 3. 4. He I say, that observes all this, cannot but be apprehensive, that *Schism* is a Sin of the *deepest* Dye and the *greatest Guilt*, and tho' the *Laws* of *Toleration* may exempt the Persons of *Schismaticks* from any *Penal Prosecution*, yet the *evil Nature* of *Schism* still continues, and cannot be alter'd by any *Humane Laws* and *Constitutions*; because *Schism* is a *Transgression* of a *Divine Positive Law*, which *God* hath made for the *Preservation* of the *Body Politick* of the *Church*, to which *Schism* is as *destructive*, as *Rebellion* to the *State*. And according to this *Principle, Donatism* and *Novatianism*, as well as *Arianism* were counted as *damnable Schisms*, under the Reigns of those Emperors who granted *Toleration* to them, as under the Reigns of those who made *Laws* against them. So that the *Breaking* of the *Church*'s *Peace* was al-

always accounted *peculiarly finful,*
when without any *just* and *necessary*
Grounds, *Contentions* did run fo
high, as to appear in an open *Schism*
and *Separation.* And tho' *Separa-*
tion is both *lawful* and *necessary,* and
free from the *Sin* of *Schism,* where
Communion cannot be kept without
Sin ; yet the *Writings* of all the *Apo-*
stolical and *Ancient Fathers* do condemn and aggravate the *Sin* of *unne-*
cessary Separation. St. *Ignatius* the
fecond Bishop of *Antioch,* in Succeffion from St. *Peter,* in his Epiftles
ad Trallianos, ad Smyrneufes, and
in thofe to the *Philippians, Ephefians*
and *Philadelphians* frequently requires them to keep themfelves in
the *Unity* and *Communion* of the *Chri-*
stian Church, by a *regular Obedience*
to the *Bishops,* and by a *Communica-*
tion with the *Priefts,* who were fet
over them by the *Authority* of *Epi-*
fcopal Order: and to *difobey* thofe
Bishops and their *Presbyters,* and to
feparate from them, is in thofe Epi-

ftles

files charg'd with *Schism.* And 'tis a known and approv'd Saying of *Dionysius Alexandrinus, That to suffer Martyrdom* ἕνεκεν τὸ μὴ χίσαι *rather than to divide the Church by* Schism, *is not less glorious than to be a Martyr for refusing to offer Sacrifice unto Idols (b).* To these we may add St. *Cyprian* the worthy Bishop of *Carthage,* who in his Fortieth Epistle *ad Populum Carthaginensem de quinque Presbyteris Schismaticis,* exhorts them to have no *Communion* with those who had divided themselves from their *Bishops*; for he tells them in that Epistle, That to be *sine Episcopis,* without *Bishops,* was to be *extra Ecclesiam,* without the *Church.* And in his Book *de Unitate,* he gives us this Notion of *Schism, Contemptis Episcopis & derelictis Dei Sacerdotibus constituere aliud Altare, aut Conventicula diversa constituere:* That it was *Schism* to contemn and

(b) *Euseb. Eccl. Hist. l. 6. c. 42.*

for-

forsake the *Bishops*, and *Priests* 'of
God, and to set up another *Altar*, or
to settle distinct *Conventicles*. In
the very same Book he also asserts
that the *Sin* of breaking the *Church*'s
Peace by *Schism*, is in divers Respects
more hainous than the *Sin* of those
lapsed *Christians*, who in the time
of *Persecution*, yielded to offer Sacrifice to Idols. Because the latter
lamented his great *Infirmity*, and by
his *Repentance* sought for Pardon
from *God*, and *Communion* with his
Church, his *straits* and *dangers* were
the Causes of his *Crime*, and though
he miscarry'd himself, he did not al-
lure and perswade others into the
same *Transgression*, but might afterwards be honour'd as a *Martyr:*
Whereas the former was *swelling* and
pleasing himself in his *Sin*, did di-
sturb, oppose and reject the *Church*,
his *Sin* was of his own free and vo-
luntary *Choice*, and he also *beguil'd*
and *ensnar'd* others. And all this
was express'd by these two last mention'd

on'd Writers, with peculiar reference to the *Novatian Schism*, which then made a *Breach* in the *Church*'s *Unity*, about matters of *Discipline*, without denying any *Articles* of the *Faith*. And then St. *Cyprian* proceeds so far as to declare, That if the Man who sows *Discord* in the *Church* should lay down his Life in the Defence of the Name of *Christ*, the stain of his *Sin* could not be wip'd out (that is so as to render him honoured in the *Church*) by the stream of his *Blood*, but as he goes on, *Inexpiabilis & gravis est culpa discordiæ, nec passione purgatur*, That *Martyrdom* it self cannot expiate the *Guilt* of *Schism* (c). I tremble to think what a *dreadful Aggravation* of the Condition of the *Damned* it is, that they are *banish'd* from the *Presence* of the *Lord*, and from the *Glory* of his *Power*. The same is their *Condition* also who are *disunited* from *Je-*

(c) *Cyp. de Unit. Ecclef.*

sus

sus Christ by being *disunited* from his *visible Representative* the *Bishop*. They can have none of that *Peace* which passeth all Understanding, who are no Subjects of the Prince of *Peace*, nor Members of his *Kingdom*. They can have no *Visitations* of the *Heavenly Spirit*, who are divided from that *Body* of which the *Spirit* is the *Bond* and *Cement*. And, which is the most *piercing* and *dreadful Reflection* of all, this *miserable Condition* cuts them off from those *future Expectations*, which are the only *Supports* and *Alleviations* of *good Men* in this Life under their *severest Sufferings*. They then who are *disunited* from *Jesus Christ* in this World, have no Hopes of recovering an *Union* with him hereafter in the World to come. It is very certain, that in whatsoever Condition they shall die, in that they must abide to all *Eternity*. And how *disconsolate* and *deplorable* must it seem to any *Soul*,

that

that it muſt want the *Comforts* of *Religion* here, and loſe the *Hopes* of enjoying them everlaſtingly hereafter? Let all Perſons then have an eſpecial Care, that they do not in any wiſe attempt the *overturning* and *abrogating* the *Sacred Order* of *Epiſcopacy*, which was *Eſtabliſh'd* by *Chriſt* in his *Church*, For 'tis no leſs than a *Sacrilegious Robbing* the *Church* of that *Miniſtry*, which *Chriſt* in his *infinite Wiſdom* thought neceſſary for her *Edification* and *Perfection*. You know what a *dreadful Curſe* is pronounc'd againſt them, who either add to, or take away from the *Inſtitutions* of *Jeſus Chriſt*, *Rev.* 22. 18, 19. I know 'tis pretended by ſome, that (in the preſent State of the *Church*) *Dioceſan Epiſcopacy* may be laid aſide, and that the *Church* may be as well *Govern'd* by *Presbyters*, and therefore it is needleſs to keep up any *Diſtinction of Offices*. But is not this to pretend to be

wi-

wifer than *Jesus Christ?* Is not this
to confound and jumble together the
different *Orders Instituted* by him?
Is not this to fet up a new *Model*
different from what he not only
Establish'd, but also appointed to
continue in his *Church* to the End
of the World? Is not this to cafhier
Christ's Prime Officers and *Reprefen-*
tatives, and the *Church's Principal*
Guides? In fhort, Is not this to
rend and tear from the *Church* the
Pledges of our *Saviour's Care* and
Kindnefs which he beftow'd upon
her, when he Afcended up into *Hea-*
ven? And now in the Clofe of this
Difcourfe, I do heartily advife all thofe
Schifmaticks, who ftill wander from
the *Fold,* and walk in bye and for-
bidden *Paths,* that they would now
return to the *Shepherd* and *Bifhop*
of their *Souls,* and that they would
confefs in the Words of our *Church,*
That, *They have erred and strayed*
from God's ways like loft Sheep: And
fince

fince many of them have left the *Publick Prayers* of the *Church*, for the *Private Conceptions* of Men's Brains, they have great Reafon to fay, That, *They have followed too much the Devices and Defires of their own Hearts.* Beware then how you turn your Backs upon thofe *incomparable Prayers* and *Confeffions* in our *Liturgy*, which are fo well adapted to the *Wants* and *Neceffities* of your *Souls*: But do you fet a Value upon that *ineftimable Treafury* of *Piety* and *Devotion*; in the Ufe of which, you may be furnifh'd with all *Divine Bleffings*, neceffary for the *Life* that now is, and that which is to come.

How happy then fhould I be, if I might prevail with you to be *reconcil'd* to our Moft *Excellent Church*, and to frequent our *Publick Affemblies*, where *God* is *greatly Reverenc'd*, in our *Approaches*
to

to *Him*, with the *humble* and *decent Gestures* of our Bodies. O then may we all of us so *unite* in one *Fellowship* and *Communion* here upon *Earth*, that we may be hereafter Translated into the ever-blessed *Society* and *Communion* of *Saints* in *Heaven*.

.

F I N I S.

Books lately Printed for *W. Freeman*, againſt the *Middle-Temple-Gate, Fleetſtreet.*

A Compleat Hiſtory of *England*, with the Lives of all the Kings and Queens thereof, from the Earlieſt Account of Time, to the Death of his late Majeſty King *William* III. Written by Mr. *John Allton*, *S. Daniel*, Eſq; *J. Habington*, Eſq; Sir *T. Moore*, *G. Buck*, Eſq; the Lords *Bacon* and *Herbert*, Sir *J. Hayward*, Biſhop *Godwin*, *W. Camden*, Eſq, *J. Wilſon*, Eſq; and the Four laſt Reigns by a Learned and Impartial Hand.) Containing a Faithful Relation of all Affairs of State Eccleſiaſtical and Civil. The whole Illuſtrated with large and uſeful Notes, taken from divers Manuſcripts and other good Authors, And the Effigies of the Kings and Queens from the Originals, Engraven by the beſt Maſters. In Three Vol. in *Folio.*

New Obſervations on the Natural Hiſtory of this World of Matter, and this World of Life. Being a Philoſophical Diſcourſe, grounded upon the *Moſaick Syſtem* of the *Creation* and the *Flood*, with ſome Thoughts concerning *Paradice*, the *Conflagration of the World.* A Treatiſe of *Meteorology*, and ſome occaſional Remarks upon ſome late *Theories, Conferences* and *Eſſays. Pr.* 2s 6d

The *Anatomy of the Earth*, 4to *Price* 2s. 6d. Theſe two writ by *T. Robinſon*, Rector of *Ousby* in *Cumberland.*

A Diſcourſe of *Natural* and *Reveal'd Religion.* By *T. Nourſe*, 8vo, *Price* 2s. 6d.

A Diſcourſe concerning the *Certainty* of a *Future* and *Immortal State*, in ſome Moral, Phiſiological and Religious Conſiderations. By a *Doctor of Phyſ. Pr.* 2s. 6d.

Juſt Publiſh'd, A Third Edition of *Bond's Compleat Guide* for a *Juſtice of Peace*, Carefully Revis'd, Corrected, new Methodiz'd and continu'd down to the End of the laſt Seſſions of Parliament, 1706. To which is likewiſe added two Orders of Seſſions, one for limiting the Rate of Servants Wages, ſeveral Artificers and Labourers, the other for ſettling the Rate of Carriers for carrying of Goods, with ſeveral other Additions and large Improvements, never before Printed in any Book of this kind: And a new Table. By *J. W.* of the *Middle-Temple, Barriſter. Price* 6s.

Lightning Source UK Ltd.
Milton Keynes UK
UKHW022035160720
366673UK00013B/276